The Bobbin Lace Manual

The Bobbin Lace Manual

Geraldine Stott

B.T. Batsford Ltd · London

ISBN 0 7134 5511 X

Printed in Hong Kong
for the publisher
B.T. Batsford Ltd
4 Fitzhardinge Street
London W1H 0AH

Acknowledgement

Without the help and support of my husband, students and friends, this latest book would never have been possible. As usual my beginner class have tested all the patterns, and have given valuable advice and encouragement. Special thanks to David Minchin for the photographs and to Anne Erdman for patiently correcting my spelling and grammar.

Contents

○ Introduction 7
⊛ Beginning bobbin lace 8
⊛ First basic pillow 9
⊛ Worker cloth 9
● Abbreviations and symbols 10
● Colour-coding 10
⊛ Bobbin lore 11
⊛ Getting ready 12
⊛ Bobbin winding 13
⊛ Lacemakers' Magic Knot 13
○ Introducing colour coding in diagrams 15
● Wholestitch and halfstich 16
● Footsides; veining; braiding 18
⊛ Putting your pillow to bed 20
⊛ Carrying bags 20
⊛ Basic bobbin carrier 20
⊛ Pin talk 21
⊛ Modern prickings 22
○ Work sequence notes 23
● 1 Poppies bookmark sampler – temporary pinholes and hanging-on in order 24
● What lace? 28
● Lace language 29
⊛ Handy hints 30
● 2 Ninepin lace – winky pins, lazy joins and picots 32
⊛ Simple bobbin winder 36
⊛ Thread thoughts 38
● 3 Torchon fan – torchon ground, hanging on in prs, twisted ws fan 40
● Setting up or moving your lace 43
⊛ Traditional pincushion 44
⊛ Bobbin carrier 45
● 4 3D Flowers – gimps, adding in and throwing out 46
○ General instructions for starting bookmarks 48
● 5 Daisy bookmark – fans and spiders 49
● 6 Love-in-a-mist bookmark – Brabant ground 52
● 7 Lobelia bookmark – rose ground and mini-spiders 53
● 8 Bluebell bookmark – variations on a theme 54
● Spiders galore 55
● Six-pair crossings 56
● 9 Modern Bedfordshire 'leaves' 57
● Hook or needlepin sewings 58

- Summary of modern pillow types   59
- 10 Ethel medallion – using 6-pr crossings, leaves and finishing off   60
- Starting lines and finishing off   63
- Turning a corner   64
- Designing corners   65
- 11 June hanky – corners and finishing off   66
- Finishing off your hanky   68
- Block pillows   69
- 12 Torchon sampler – drawing-out exercise   70
- Eight-pair crossings   74
- Mushroom-type pillow   75
- Janice photograph-frame sampler – various fillings and designing   76
- Rescuing a disaster   80
- Bookmark tops and tails   82
- 14 Running river – Bedfordshire trails, changing workers   84
- 15 Amanda hanky – hs trails   86
- 16 French fan lavender bag – colour and French fan   87
- Square starts   88
- Square finishings   89
- 17 Linette mobile – planning-ahead exercise   90
- Picot survey   94
- 18 Bells for all occasions – interesting start and finish   96
- Trail crossings   98
- 19 Crossroads bookmark – crossing trials and unusual spiders   99
- 20 Table setting   Napkin corner   100
- 21 Table setting   Glass coasters   101
- 22 Table setting   Placemat edge   102
- 23 Table setting   Tablecloth edging   103
- 24 Table setting   Insertion   104
- Identifying four typical English laces   108
- 25 Moira locket design – RH picots   111
- 26 Annette paperweight   113
- External corners survey   114
- Internal corners survey   115
- 27 Butterfly in modern bobbin tape lace   117
- ⅛" or 3mm graph paper for Torchon sampler (page 70)   118
- Lacemakers' golden rules   119
- Books to read   120
- Suppliers and useful addresses   121
- Index   127

Introduction

Too many lacemakers learn how to make 'pure', 'traditional' lace without deviation or thought, relying entirely on their teachers, books and existing patterns.

There is so much more enjoyment to be had if lacemakers realize from an early stage that it is possible to *experiment and change* to their hearts' delight and produce something very much their own work, *not* an exact replica of thousands of other identical products.

I hope you will work ALL the patterns up to the Running River (p.84) in sequence – that way you will absorb most of the essential lacemaking techniques. The patterns have been set out in order of difficulty and each 'lesson' introduces at least one new lacemaking skill.

Thereafter I have included a variety of further patterns you should be able to tackle with your new-found expertise without too much difficulty.

I have deliberately constructed this book in an unusual way because I have found that there are many lacemakers, like myself, who skim through the valuable introductory chapters to get the bare essentials, so they can start immediately: they regrettably *very rarely look back*. So I have scattered the valuable basic knowledge that is essential to good lacemaking, and also some fascinating folklore, traditions and 'know-how', between each 'lesson'.

There are basically four different types of pages interspersed throughout this book:
1. Lesson explanation – please read these pages carefully before starting (page corners coded white).
2. Lessons proper – all clearly set out so no page turning necessary (page corners coded red).
3. Useful information – handy hints, how to make basic equipment, etc. (page corners coded grey).
4. Essential reference – those pages you will need to refer to throughout your lacemaking life (page corners coded blue).

ALL COLOUR-CODED FOR EASY REFERENCE!

Beginning bobbin lace

In this book I hope to introduce you to Bobbin Lace, also called Pillow Lace or Bone Lace. The reasons for these names will become apparent in the next few pages. Making bobbin lace is the most fascinating hobby I know because:

1. You never stop learning.
2. Unlike many handicrafts, it always looks attractive and 'different' even when not in use.
3. Antique lace is a rewarding field for the collector.

You can keep costs to a minimum, gradually building up bobbins and fancy equipment as you progress, and as birthday and Christmas money allows.

To start making lace you will need:
1. Basic pillow: see page 9.
2. Twelve pairs (24) bobbins with beads: see page 11.
3. Pins: traditionally brass 27 x ·65mm, but any rustproof pins will do.
4. Card: about the thickness of cornflake packets, but in some colour dark enough for your threads to show up clearly.
5. Thread: sewing *cotton* in many different colours. Never use pure manmade fibres: they are too stretchy and invariably collapse as soon as the pins have been removed. .
6. Cotton material to cover your pillow: see page 9.

Other threads used in this book are: Brok 36, Brok 60, DMC Coton Perlé 8, Bouc Linen 30, Bockens Linen 50/2, 18/3 and 120/2; all these should be available from suppliers of lacemaking equipment and materials (a list is given at the end of the book).

This book is an introduction to bobbin lace with details on the making of Torchon, Bedfordshire, and Braided or Modern Laces. Honiton and Bucks Point lace are rather more advanced, and so fall outside the scope of this book.

First basic pillow

Easiest and cheapest to make and use until you know if you like lacemaking enough to invest in more permanent versions. See pages 59, 69 and 75 for other types.

Use high-density polystyrene (obtainable from most building merchants as lagging).

Approx 46 x 40 x 5cm.

Cut away sides – *never* work on completely flat pillows.

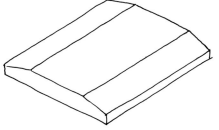

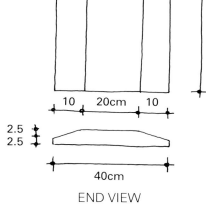

46cm

10 | 20cm | 10

2.5
2.5

40cm

END VIEW

Now polystyrene *must* be covered and 'dressed'.

Traditionally plain darkish blue or green smooth cotton should be used.

Wrap one piece completely round, turn in raw edges and pin all round.

Pin at sides, not underneath (could scratch tabletops).

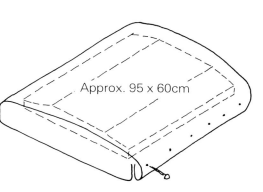

Approx. 95 x 60cm

Worker cloth

Approx 25cm x 42cm.

Ideally this edge, the edge marked with an arrow, should be as flat as possible: therefore use selvedge edge or 'wonderwebbed' hem.

Hem other three sides.

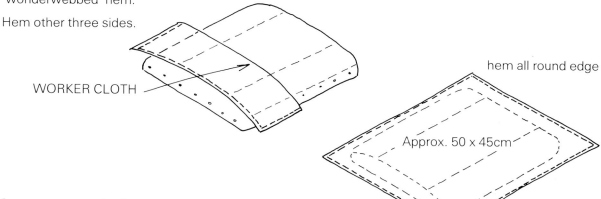

WORKER CLOTH

hem all round edge

Approx. 50 x 45cm

Large cover cloth

This covers all whenever you are not working.

Very strict rule of mine – protect the work from dirt and dust.

I recommend you copy this page and use it as a bookmark
until you get used to these abbreviations and colour-coding.
Abbreviations are necessary to keep all instructions clear and
to keep wording to a minimum.

Abbreviations and symbols

ws = wholestitch

hs = halfstitch

⊙ = temporary pinholes

pr = pair

wpr = worker pair

ppr = passive pair

tw = twist (right over left)

R = right

L = left

RHP/LHP = right hand pair/
left hand pair

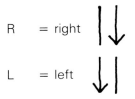

LHP   RHP

⊡ = sewing pinhole

gimp start = ▼ = pair

= ▶ = single gimp

gimp finish = ⌣

Colour coding

N.B. Each line on diagrams equals one pair

Red = wholestitch = continuous line in black-and-white diagrams

Blue = halfstitch = broken line in black-and-white diagrams

✗ = little ticks = number of twists

⋎ = throw out a pair at this point

Instructions in notes refer to the latest worker pair unless
otherwise stated (e.g. ws through ppr tw2 = wholestitch
worker pair through passive pairs, twist worker pair twice).

10

Bobbin lore

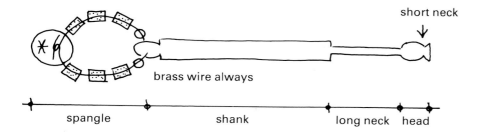

short neck

brass wire always

spangle · shank · long neck · head

Bobbins are those delightful little tools you use to make lace. They are made in wood, bone and plastic – buy the cheapest to begin with. The type, size and variety is enormous. There are many excellent modern bobbin makers now – see suppliers list at the back of the book.

These are some points to look for when choosing your bobbins. The *head and neck* MUST BE SMOOTH; there is nothing worse than rough wood, where your threads catch all the time. If you have a bobbin that catches, rub in a twisting motion with fine wire wool and furniture polish – magic!

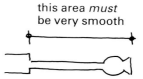

this area *must* be very smooth

Next it is advisable to choose *long, long necks*, so plenty of thread can be wound on to the bobbin. One day you will wish to make a large amount of lace!!

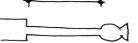

long rather than short

The bobbins I prefer and recommend have a circle of *Beads*, called 'spangles', at the bottom – this prevents the bobbins rolling and untwisting the thread, holds them in position and also gives a slight weight to help your tension. Spangles are not generally found on bobbins used in Continental Europe. It is not a good idea to mix beaded and non-beaded bobbins.

Modern spangling
(not too many or too large)

Traditional bottom beads have fascinating names – Venetian, Dolly Vardens, Kitty Fishers, Ostrich Plumes and Evil Eyes. Sometimes you will find a waistcoat or shoe button attached – all pillows should have a button on them to bring good luck.

Bobbins come in all sizes, thicknesses and lengths. You will soon find your own preference.

Start with the bare minimum (12 pairs for the first 6 lessons); gradually buy more as you progress – less painful *and*, more important, you will not end up with bobbins you find with experience you dislike using.

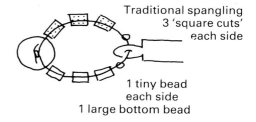

Traditional spangling
3 'square cuts'
each side

1 tiny bead
each side
1 large bottom bead

Antique bobbins are beautiful and a great investment but expensive – see the list at the back of the book for suppliers.

Getting ready

First you must make your pricking (this is equivalent to your knitting pattern)

Photocopy or trace the pricking in the book – photocopying is permissible if for your own use.

Cut out *pricking* near outside dots (*a*).

Cut *card* slightly larger than pricking (*b*).

Then, stick pricking to card with sticky tape (*c*), down one side only.

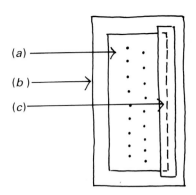

For a first basic pricker (later you can buy more sophisticated versions), use a fine sewing needle (No. 8 ideal), stuck head-first into a cork.

Prick a hole in the card at each dot marked.

Always hold your pricker at 90° to the pricking (essential to keep good clear holes): it is very, very important to spend time and be very accurate – YOUR WORK WILL DEPEND ON A GOOD, TRUE PRICKING.

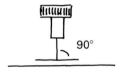

When you have pricked all the holes and *before removing* the tape, hold your pricking up to the light – this will show whether you have forgotten any holes.

Next open flap and copy onto the card from the original pricking *all the markings* and letterings in very fine pen.

Remove tape and photocopy from the card.

Attach card/pricking to pillow.

Pin pricking to the centre of the pillow as near the top as comfortable (*d*).

Pin at all four corners.

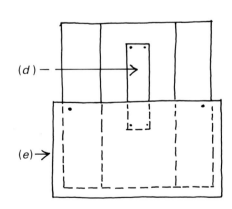

The worker cloth should be pinned tightly over bottom half of pricking (*e*).

Bobbin winding

Next you must *wind your thread* onto your bobbins. Hold first bobbin horizontally in left hand, wind thread round long neck.

Always wind thread away from yourself.

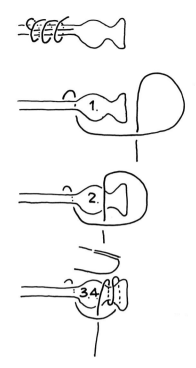

Lacemakers' Magic Knot

After you have wound on enough thread, make knot over small neck.

1. Twist thread to form a 'P'.

2. Move vertical thread to front of small neck.

3. Twist this loop twice (again away from yourself), round small neck.

4. Lightly put index finger of LH over top of this knot and gently pull loose thread to tighten knot with RH.

BOBBINS ARE ALWAYS WOUND IN PAIRS
All patterns in this book give the number of pairs needed.

Leave a gap of approx 30cm between bobbins – later with experience you will find your own ideal length preference.

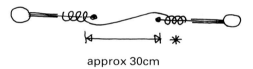

approx 30cm

Never touch your thread UNLESS ABSOLUTELY NECESSARY.

In an ideal world it is best to have all your bobbins at the same length: this not only looks impressive, but does help improve your tension.

ALWAYS WATCH YOUR WORK *not* your bobbins, then hopefully you will see mistakes as they happen and correct them immediately instead of hours later!!! What is more, you will be less likely to get 'Lacemakers' Neckache'!

To lengthen your threads, hold bobbin at 90° to thread and gently turn anti-clockwise until length is correct.

to lengthen threads

Always work with your pillow on a slope. Comfort is your first priority: soon you will find your favourite position.

Two suggestions: (*a*) using a table with the pillow resting on a book. If the table is too high, (*b*) may be more comfortable, with the pillow resting on your lap and the table edge. Make sure each time the slope is correct. Bobbins will not stay in place if the slope is too great.

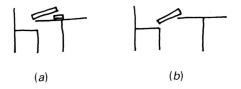

(*a*)   (*b*)

14

Introducing colour-coding in diagrams

A B C D E F J

G

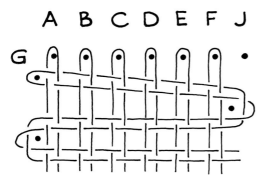

Wholestitch = WS

ONE LINE = ONE PAIR

A B C D E F J
1 1 1 1 1 1

G

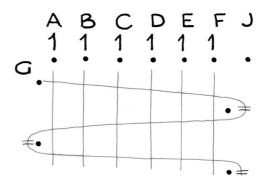

WS diagram

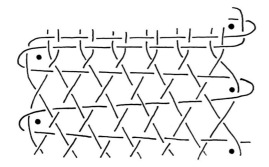

Halfstitch = HS

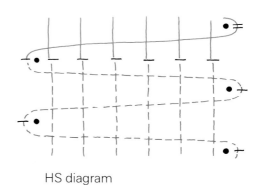

HS diagram

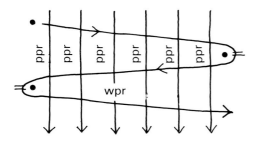

worker pair (wpr) = pair working back
and forth through passive pairs (pprs)

Numbers = no. of pairs to be hung on that pin

Red or continuous lines = ws

Blue or broken lines = hs

Ticks = number of twists

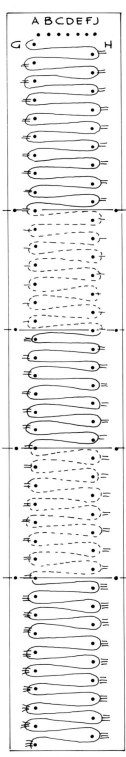

Pricking

Wholestitch
(also called 'linen stitch' and 'cloth stitch')
and
halfstitch
(also called 'lattice stitch')

7 prs bobbins

Continuous lines = wholestitch (ws); draw them in RED on this diagram and follow the box opposite.

Broken lines = halfstitch (hs); draw them in BLUE on this diagram and follow the box opposite.

Little dashes = number of twists (right over left).

START Make pricking as explained on page 12. Draw in 4 division lines on pricking as shown (left).
Put pins in holes marked *A – G*.

Select 7 *different sewing cotton colours*.

Wind 6 prs with 50cm per bobbin and hang on pins *A* to *F*.

Wind 1 pr with 150cm per bobbin and hang on pin *G*. This pair will be very busy and will be called the worker pair.

Now work ws and hs as colours indicate: see notes opposite.

Please practise these two basic stitches until they become second nature. Ignore the rude comments from the family about the time it takes to make tartan bandage: *very soon*, I promise, they will be very impressed with your REAL lace.

Remember all lace beginners learn to unpick much faster than going forwards!!!

Finishing off: Elongate all threads to about 20cm by unwinding the bobbins. Divide wpr and tie knot round last pin. (You will find it easier to put beads first through loop.) Tie off all passives in pairs. Cut off bobbins.

Removing pins: Leave top 6 pins and bottom 2 pins, gently remove all other pins, then remove top and bottom pins. TAKE CARE WITH HS – it is very unstable and if accidently pulled, will end up like a bootlace!!

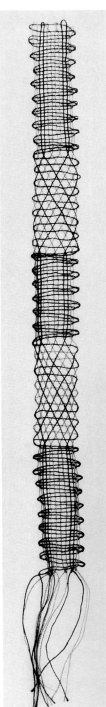

Wholestitch:
abbreviated to ws and coloured RED on diagrams.

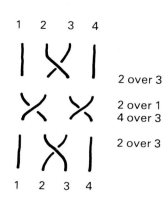

2 over 3

2 over 1
4 over 3

2 over 3

> WHOLESTITCH = 2 over 3
> 2 over 1 *and* 4 over 3 (worked as one
> 2 over 3 — using both hands)

Numbers refer to positions *not* bobbins. Always count from left to right.

With pr from G and pr from A work ws; after first ws ignore LHP and push it to left of pillow; work ws with RHP and next pr to right, repeat until right hand edge (H).

At edge twist last pr twice (tw2) right over left, stick pin under RHP (worker pr). Stroke/pull passive threads* so they hang vertical and straight.

Now you are ready to return, working exactly as above except ws with wpr and pr to left, reject RHP and push to right of pillow.

TWIST = ALWAYS RIGHT OVER LEFT

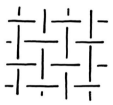

wholestitch = woven/linen look

Halfstitch

Abbreviated to hs and coloured BLUE on diagrams.

For this exercise, twist each passive pr before starting hs sections.

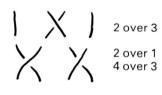

2 over 3

2 over 1
4 over 3

> HALFSTITCH = 2 over 3
> 2 over 1 *and* 4 over 3 as above

Work hs across to right as you did in ws.

At edge twist wpr only once (note hs already has one twist).

If you get *lost in hs* which often happens, the only answer for a beginner is to undo the row until the last pin completed (making sure all pprs are twisted) and start that row again; with practice you will eventually get to know how, without going back so frequently!

Experiment with different numbers of twists at the edge of the next two sections and observe the difference – the worker is constant in ws, but in hs the workers change all the time with an even number of twists.

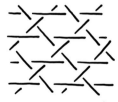

halfstitch = horizontal lines with x's between

* Stroking your *bobbins* (not the threads) in a gentle downwards motion helps settle and straighten your pprs and also lets you pause to check all is correct.

Footsides; veining; braiding

9 prs (6 short and 3 long) Many colours again

On page 16 I mentioned that halfstitch was very unstable; in this pattern you will learn to put an edge to your lace which will stabilize it.

(a)

Footsides: Straight edges to give finish and strength to the sides of the lace and used for sewing to fabrics. The straight footside is *always on the right* in BRITISH LACE.

There are basically two types of footsides:

(b)

1. *pin under one* (as first example): work to outside edge, twist, pin under one pr, and return.

2. *pin under two* (most frequently used): work to one pr before outside edge, twist, ws through outside edge pr, pin under two prs and return with new wpr.

(c)

(d)

It will become obvious after a few rows, that the workers change in a sequence; see if you can spot it. This is the advantage of working in multiple colours – you will be able to observe and note if you have got it right!

(a) ws in the middle
(b) hs in the middle
Veining: Simple way to create a design by just extra twists of the threads.

(e)

(c) 3ws – tw3 – 3ws
(d) 2ws – tw2 – 2ws – tw2 – 2ws
(e) ws and twist both wpr and ppr
Braiding: Continuous hs – used a great deal in Bedfordshire and Torchon Laces.

(f)

(f) braiding finished off with overhand knot.

KEEP A NOTEBOOK AND ALL YOUR SAMPLES!
For future reference the most valuable attempts are the ones that went wrong.

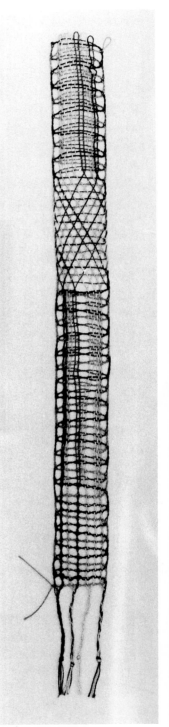

Footsides; veining; braiding (cont.)

9 prs (6 short and 3 long) Many colours again

Use the same pricking as the first exercise.
Hang bobbins on *A* to *F* (short threads)
Hang 1 long pr on *J*

Starting round a pin: hang 2 long prs *in order* on *G*, twl LHP and tw2 RHP; hs through each other, twl both – see diagram.

Footsides: leave LHP, take second pr from outside;
* ws through all remaining prs except the last pr, tw2 the wpr (the pr travelling horizontally), ws through last pr, *pin under both* outside prs, tw2 both; reject the old wpr (outside pr) and now you are ready to ws back to the other side using your new wpr*

Repeat from * to *.

> Footside stitch = tw2, ws, pin under both, tw2 both

Halfstitch with footings: when you feel confident with ws in the middle, try a patch of hs.

Next experiment with Veining – with just a few twists of the wprs it is possible to achieve some very interesting effects in the ws.

Divide your passives into 2 equal groups, in this case 3 and 3. Ws through the first group of passives, tw3 the wpr, then ws through the second group of 3 passives, work footsides as before. After a few more rows you will note a ladder effect running up the middle. Later when you have time and more confidence, you can experiment putting the twists in different places – see sample. When you reach the end of your pricking, finish off this time with braids.

Separate the 2 threads of the last wpr, take threads each side of the last pin and tie a reef knot round the pin and cut off. Then divide all your bobbins into 4 groups of 2 prs.

> Braiding = continuous hs

Working 2 prs at a time, make continuous half-stitches one after the other without pinning, pulling it tight by gently separating the prs every other stitch.

G

hanging on in order	tw1 LHP tw2 RHP

hs, tw1 both

Joining two prs round a pin

Footside stitch

Braiding

Putting your pillow to bed

Whenever the pillow is to be moved or it is not in use, it is imperative to anchor the bobbins firmly in place – you will be amazed at the muddle they will get into if not fastened down.

Secure with 1cm elastic pinned at frequent intervals with berry pins between bobbins (a).

Fold and pin worker cloth up to catch any escaping bobbins (b).

Then cover all with large cover cloth (c).

It is very, very important to cover your pillow and work at all times when not in use (I forgot the other day whilst working in the garden, and stopped for a coffee: yes – you can guess what flew over and redecorated my work!). Dust also is a great problem.

I always recommend you put your cover on your lap whilst working, then when you get up, obviously you will put your cover on!!

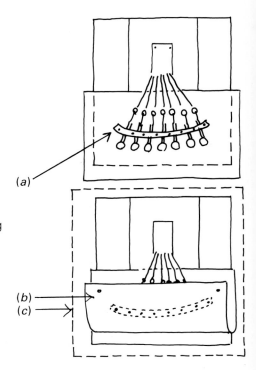

(a)

(b)
(c)

Carrying bags (simple to make)

zips or Velcro sides (d)

pillow size (e)

good idea to stop zips and just sew last 10cm (catchment area for escapee pins, bobbins, threads etc) (f)

check overall length (bag + handle): the bag will drag on the floor if too long.

If bag + handle is too long, I suggest you make the handle longer to become a shoulder strap.

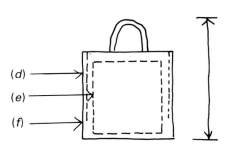

(d)
(e)
(f)

Basic bobbin carrier (for ready wound prs)

A very easy and cheap system – using an old cereal box and thick elastic bands; it can be refined by putting a weight at the bottom of box and covering with sticky-backed felt.

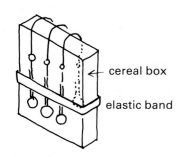

← cereal box

elastic band

Pin talk

Both sets of *edge pins* must slope outwards. Lace has a tendency to work up the pins otherwise.

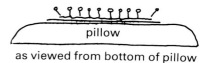

pillow

as viewed from bottom of pillow

Try also to slope the *middle pins* very slightly backwards (away from you).

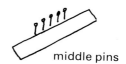

middle pins

In the past lacemakers attached goose-grass seeds to the heads of the *foot- and headside pins*; it is good to follow tradition and use berrypins or sealing-waxed pins.

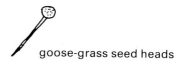

goose-grass seed heads

Strivers were very pretty extra long pins with tiny beads halfway up them. They were used in the past to gauge the time taken to produce a length of lace.

striver

There's no need for a whole boxful of pins in your work — it is essential to keep top and side pins in as long as possible but you only need about 5cm depth of pins in the middle.

N.B. Leave your lace to 'set' in all its pins for at least 24 hours.
If you can bear it, it is well worth it.

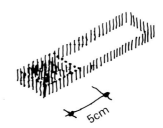

5cm

. . . you only need 5cm depth of pins

When you have finished your first effort, great care must be taken when *removing pins*. Try not to touch your work too much; it cannot be avoided entirely — so make sure your hands are extra-clean.

Carefully remove central pins first, then the edge pins; lastly top and bottom pins.

Modern prickings

The method shown first is ideal and looks more authentic but . . . from experience I find there are many lacemakers who have neither pens, skills nor time to prick and draw out complicated patterns.

The following is the method I use constantly:

1. Photocopy your pattern (legal only for your own personal use).

2. Cut out card slightly larger.

3. Cover pricking and card with sticky-backed *coloured* transparent plastic film.

4. Rub with wire wool to remove the shine if necessary – a matt version is also now available.

It is still essential to use card underneath – I have seen several disasters where paper + film have crinkled, creating an unacceptably poor pricking.

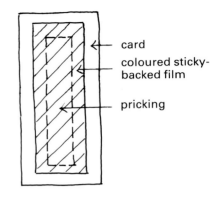

card

coloured sticky-
backed film

pricking

Work sequence notes

Here are some general principles to follow: they will become clearer as you work through pages 24-26.

Bobbin laces are invariably worked on the diagonal. Sometimes you need to *start in a straight line* across the top. This is how you proceed. After a straight start, you have to gradually build up your diagonal line.

When a complete line is established, you work down each line in turn:

Note: YOU NEVER WORK UPHILL

Work down each line in an elongated zigzag.

For Pattern No. 1, start with 3rd pr from outside RH edge, ws through ppr, work footside, ws back through ppr; then you are ready to work down next 'row'.

Work down each diagonal line in turn, until the end, *return through ppr* and leave.

You will find in bobbin lace that you will be unable to work one area until other areas have been completed.

Here your diamond cannot be worked until the little triangle has been finished.

This triangle is worked as your diagonal lines *but* stopping one row *before* the motif — it is essential to note this point: you will find you will not be able to work your diamond if you have not stopped! This problem is guaranteed to happen sometime.

It does not matter which direction you work your diamonds, *but always the same way in one piece of lace.*

Handy hint: When you reach the bottom of diamonds you must end up with just 2 pairs round the bottom pin — any more, and you can guarantee you have forgotten to leave a pr out somewhere.

1. Poppies bookmark sampler

12 prs bobbin – Brok 36
Permutations on a theme; introducing temporary pinholes and hanging on in order

This time there are no definite working prs, so *wind each bobbin with equal amounts.* Rule of thumb for these samples: 4 times the length of finished lace.

> ☉ This symbol indicates a temporary pinhole to be used until work has begun. Please do not forget to remove as soon as possible or you will end up with little loops at the top of your completed work.
>
> ⋂ Hanging on *in order:* This method will be used throughout unless otherwise stated. That is to say:
>
> Hang first pr over pin, hang second pr outside first pr round pin.

Hang 2 prs in order on top 5 pinholes and 1 pr on each ☉ marked ☉^{1}.

At all 5 top pinholes, tw1 LHP, tw2 RHP, hs through each other, tw1 both

START TOP LH SIDE at *1* (refer to numbers on diagram opposite)

ws tw1 both through ppr (no pin)	1				
ws pin ws tw1 both	2	6-8	12-16	21-27	D-K
ws tw1 back through ppr (no pin)	3	9	17	28	L
ws tw1 both, through outside pr, extra tw1 outside pr, pin under both	4	10	18	29	M
Remove LH ☉; gently pull pr down to just touch existing threads					
ws tw1 both	5	11	19	30	N
Leave and start again RH side					
ws tw1 both through ppr (no pin)	A				
ws tw1 both through outside pr, extra tw1 outside pr, pin under both	B				

(continued on page 26)

1. Poppies bookmark sampler (cont.)

12 prs – Brok 36
Permutations on a theme; introducing temporary pinholes and hanging on in order

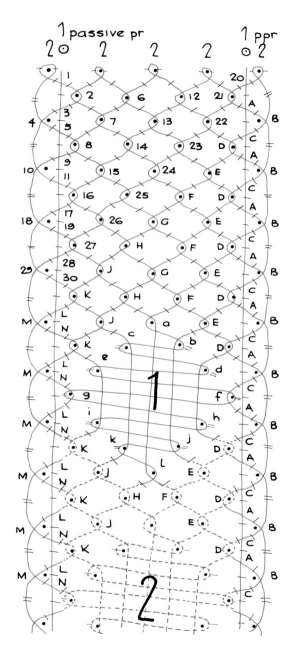

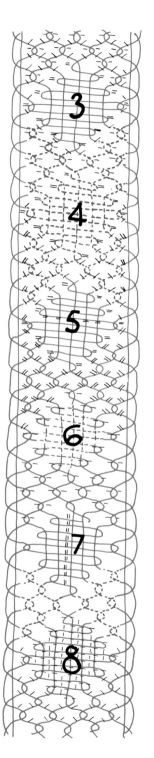

Remove RH ⊙; gently pull pr down to just touch existing threads.					
ws tw1 both through ppr (no pin)	C	20			
Continue as above from D.					

For diamond follow lower-case letters — ws back and forth picking up new pr at end of each row until widest point is reached; return through all prs *except last pr* each row.

N.B. tw2 wpr at each pinhole; tw1 all 8 prs from diamond (and after all ws diamonds).

Work diamonds and triangles as indicated on the pricking page; they should all be self explanatory except:

⬡ ws back and forth until pin *f*: tw2 all vertical pprs and continue as usual.

◇ after pin *b*, ws through 2 pprs, tw2 wpr, ws back and forth as usual *but* tw2 wpr on each row below first tw2.

1. Poppies bookmark sampler (cont.)

12 prs – Brok 36
Permutations on a theme; introducing temporary pinholes and hanging on in order

N.B. Work this sample all in WS FIRST until you are confident you understand, then have fun experimenting and trying out these permutations.

1st ground – ws pin ws tw1

1. ws, tw1 at pins

hs pin hs

2. hs, tw1 at pins

ws tw1 pin ws tw1

3. ws, tw2 at pins

hs tw1 pin hs tw1

4. hs, tw2 at pins

hs pin hs tw1

5. ws with horizontal bar

ws pin ws tw2

6. hs with ws tw1 each side of pin

ws tw1 pin ws tw2

7. ws with vertical bar

hs pin hs

8. twisted ws (ws tw1 throughout)

ws pin ws tw1

This can be made into a 'real' bookmark by using larger-scale graph paper and thicker thread.

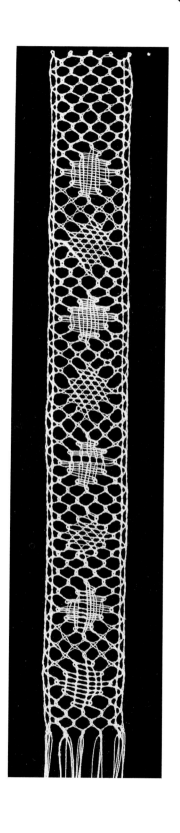

What lace?

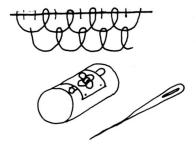

Needle lace is made with a sewing needle and fine thread — made up of many buttonhole stitches.

It is made on a little cylindrical pillow. A thick outlining thread is couched onto the pricking equivalent and then buttonholed row after row.

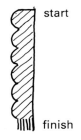

Bobbin laces are made with many bobbins and many threads.

They come in two basic types:

Continuous or straight lace

Ground and motifs etc. made at the same time.

Pillow rarely changes position. Typical examples: Torchon and Bucks Point laces.

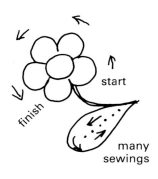

See pages 108-110 for more information.

Non-continuous or part lace

Individual motifs made separately and joined together later.

Pillow continually being moved. Typical examples: Honiton and Belgian laces.

Lace language

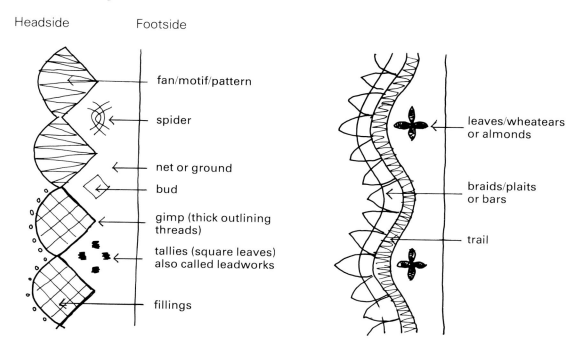

Headside   Footside

fan/motif/pattern

spider

net or ground

bud

gimp (thick outlining threads)

tallies (square leaves) also called leadworks

fillings

leaves/wheatears or almonds

braids/plaits or bars

trail

These seem to be the most popular names; there are many localized names. Each area, as with dialects, has its own and I believe they should be kept if at all possible. I suggest as you find more you write them in and build up your own collection.

Handy hints

Hold passives with one hand while pulling up the worker pair with other hand. This saves much pulling of passives after pinning; there will still be some adjusting of passives, but not as much.

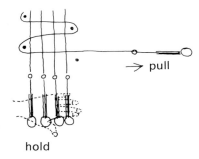

hold

Use *palm of hand* when moving a mass of bobbins from one side of pillow to other – this method helps prevent bobbins hopping over each other.

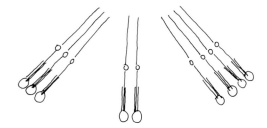

Wide working space: push the bobbins not in use to either side of the working space – you will find it much easier to work without muddle; doing so makes clear the pairs to be worked and also settles the thread round the pins, especially when working such features as spiders and fans.

Mini bean bag (approx 20 x 30cm) filled with polystyrene beads is an excellent lightweight pillow support – light to carry, and you can plump it into any desired shape.

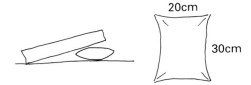

20cm

30cm

Keep a notebook. It is essential to make notes — especially of the type and size of thread. We all believe we will remember — we never do!!

Keep all your samples. You will learn much by observing your progress.

Pillow labels. How I wish this simple idea could be used universally, especially at Lace Days. Lacemaking is a continual learning process. We would all learn so much more if, when we see a thread that we liked (or disliked) we could read the label, rather than ask and be told nine times out of ten, 'I don't know — something I found in my workbox'.

```
*******************************************************
* Your name ...................................................................... *
* Name of Lace ................................................................... *
* Where pattern came from ................................................. *
* Threads used .................................................................... *
*******************************************************
```

Mistakes. There will be many — have patience. I still make mistakes; I promise they are less numerous as you progress. All beginners are expert at going backwards (I call it reverse lace!) long before they are expert at going forwards.

Please unpick — try to aim for excellence rather than yardage; it will be more satisfying in the end.

With the beaded bobbins used in Britain we work with them lying *on the pillow*, not in our hands as on the Continent.

So aim to keep bobbins as close to the pillow as possible; then your lace will not work up the pins.

Personalize your lace, *but* please make sure you understand why the original was designed the way it was.

My favourite student is the lacemaker who asks 'why'.

2. Ninepin Lace

8 prs – sewing cotton or Brok 36
Introducing: Winkie pins; Lazy Joins; Picots

Hang 2 prs on ⊙ *a, b* and *c* and start pin *A* (remember in order (⌒)).

A: tw1 LHP, tw2 RHP, hs through each other (starting round a pin)

B: ws LHP from A through 2 prs from c (footside passives) tw2

C: ws wpr through 2 prs from b, tw2 pin, ws back through prs from C, tw2

D: ws wpr through passives, tw2

E: ws wpr through outside pr, tw2 both, pin under both, leave outside pr and return with new wpr
Remove temporary pins b & c and gently pull prs into place.

F: ws wpr through passives, tw2

G: pin. This purely decorative pinhole is called a Winkie Pin.

H: as *D*

I: as *E*

J: ws wpr through passives tw2 and leave

K: braid to L (Braid = continuous hs – see page 19). Braiding will look best if you always stop just before rather than just after next pinhole.

L: LAZY JOIN with prs from *a* and K, let down

> Lazy join/windmill: Ingenious method of joining 2 sets of 2 prs round a pin.
>
> Using 2 threads as one, work as ws *but* before last 2 over 3, stick in pin then cross last 2 over 3.

M: braid to *O*

N: braid to *U*

(continued on page 34)

2. Ninepin Lace (cont.)

8 prs – sewing cotton or Brok 36
Introducing: Winkie pins; Lazy Joins; Picots
Many Bedfordshire Patterns use this design at the headside edges

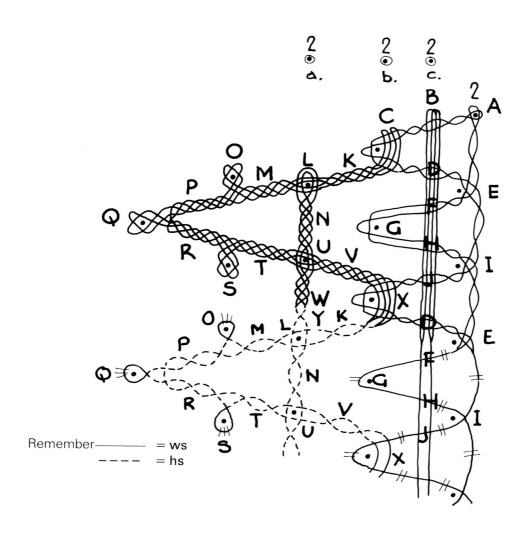

Remember ———— = ws
- - - - = hs

O: PICOT

Picots: Those pretty little loops at the headside of lace. There are many different methods and types that I will introduce later.

This method I believe is very effective and simple for the beginner:

tw3 outside pr.
Put pin on top of threads, twist pin downwards so threads twist round pin put in pin.
Separate these threads to guarantee the twists end up round the pin, tw1 outside pr.

P: braid to Q

Q: picot

R: braid to S. To guarantee a tight picot at Q – carry on making braid R in same direction until approx correct length then gently turn

S: picot

T: braid to U

U: lazy join

V: braid to X

W: braid to Y

X: ws wpr from J through 2 prs from V, tw2 pin and ws back through braid prs, tw2

Repeat from *D*, omitting ⊙ notes.

2. Ninepin Lace (cont.)

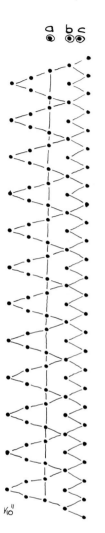

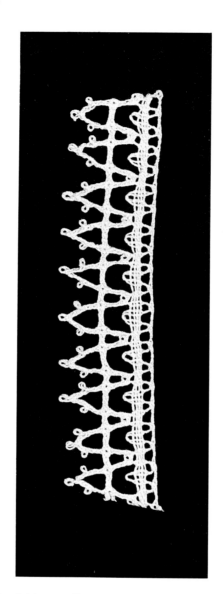

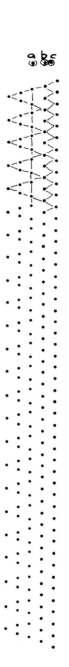

Work the left hand (large-scale) pricking until your are
confident to work smaller pricking.

Simple bobbin-winder

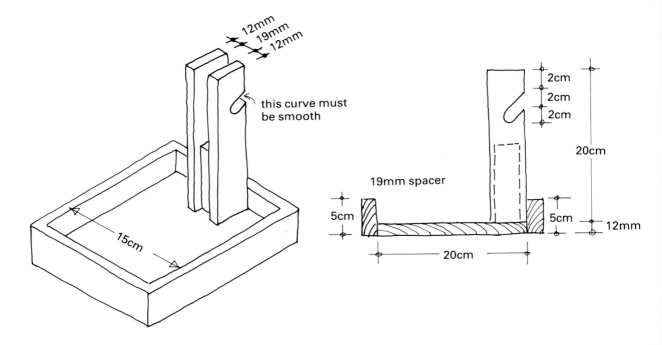

12mm
19mm
12mm

this curve must
be smooth

15cm

2cm
2cm
2cm

20cm

19mm spacer

5cm

5cm

12mm

20cm

This is a copy of a medieval Bruges winder.

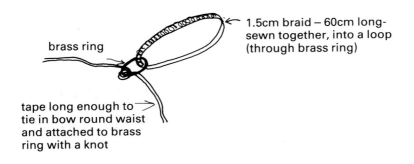

brass ring

1.5cm braid – 60cm long-
sewn together, into a loop
(through brass ring)

tape long enough to
tie in bow round waist
and attached to brass
ring with a knot

How to use it

Sit down, tie tape round waist.

Start winding bobbin by hand.

Put bobbin through braid loop; hook bobbin onto sloping ledges.

Sit back until braid is taut.

Now just pull bottom of braid to turn the bobbin in the correct direction.

Result: much better and faster than winding by hand.

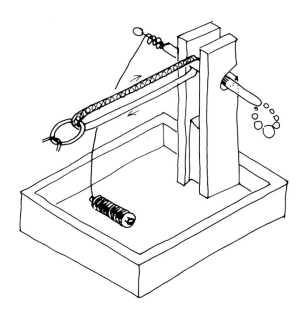

Thread thoughts

You can make lace with most threads.

Threads are always a great worry: as soon as you discover a thread you like using, it will be discontinued! I advise you to make small samples from any thread you buy, *mark them and keep them* so you have a record of the threads *you* have.

The best threads for bobbin lace are linen, cotton and silk.

LINEN is crisp in look and feel;
  slubby with different thicknesses which makes it
  unsuitable for some laces;
  more 'sticky' to work — you have to take extra care round
  pins etc. but the effort is worthwhile in the end;
  everlasting;
  full of character;
  has slubs useful for texture though not so good for
  smooth, clean lines;
  has marvellous unique texture and feel.

COTTON is the cheapest thread;
  mercerized = soft;
  glazed = hard and smooth — nearest to linen in finished
  article;
  nowadays almost as good as linen.
  Cotton threads 'slip' past each other. Choose the right
  thread for the article — soft mercerized for hankies and
  hard-glazed for household and very firm use.

SILK is a pure natural material that has a will of its own and
  needs some practice to gain control, but it is worth it in the
  end. Smooth and shiny in finish with beautiful colours.

MANMADE THREADS are to be avoided — they are too
  stretchy. Some of the cotton/manmade mixes are fairly
  good, but need thorough testing before embarking on a
  project.

Whichever threads you use take great care to match material type to thickness.

As to thickness of threads, the final decision is entirely a matter of taste. You may wish your lace to look very fine and lacey *or* not so fine and more practical.

I personally prefer the former, because it needs more skill and resembles most old laces. Thick lace can look too mechanical and machine-made if you are not careful.

Aim for muslin not sheets: we want to see individual threads not a solid mass!

NEVER pull threads from the top of spool or bobbins — this only serves to over- or under-twist the threads, and makes them unmanageable and weakens them.

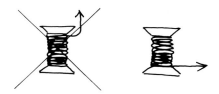

Handy hint: Mark all your thread spools with thread size or tuck the label inside the spool after it has been opened, then you will know its pedigree.

HANDLE YOUR THREADS AS LITTLE AS POSSIBLE.

3. Torchon fan (also called Fir-tree fan)

8 prs – Brok 36
Introducing: Torchon ground; hanging on in pairs; twisted ws fan

Hang 3 prs on pin *1 in pairs*

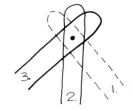

Hanging on IN PAIRS

> HANGING ON IN PAIRS – hang on a pin in sequence from R to L keeping pair threads together

Hang 1 pr on ⊙ above *2 3* & *4.*
Hang 2 prs on ⊙ above *5 in order* (one of these prs will be fan wpr, therefore wind extra thread on these prs).

1: ws RHP through other 2 prs, tw1 all 3 prs
2, 3, and *4:* hs pin hs (Torchon ground) with pr from above
         and pr from R.

Torchon Ground

> Torchon ground = hs pin hs =

5: use the 2 prs from ⊙ above as one, lazy join with pr from R, tw1 all 3 prs.

Remove all ⊙ and gently pull down to new pins.

6: Footside – ws tw1 3rd pr from outside edge through ppr and outer pr, pin under both (give extra tw1 to outside pr as usual), ws tw1 new wpr through ppr.

7 and *8:* Torchon ground with pr from above and pr from R.
9: as *6.*
10: Torchon ground
11: as *6.*
5 to *12:* ws tw 1 RHP from *5* through prs from *8* & *10;* pin under wpr, tw1 wpr
12 to *13:* 4 ws tw1, pin under wpr, tw1 wpr
13 to *14:* 3 ws tw1   „   „   „   „   „
14 to *15:* 3 ws tw1   „   „   „   „   „
15 to *16:* 2 ws tw1   „   „   „   „   „
16 to *17:* 2 ws tw1   „   „   „   „   „
17 to *18:* 5 ws tw1   „   „   „   „   „

Junction at 5.

18 to *19:* 5 *ws* tw1   „   „   „   „   „
19 to *20:* 2 ws tw1   „   „   „   „   „
20 to *21:* 2 ws tw1   „   „   „   „   „
21 to *22:* 3 ws tw1   „   „   „   „   „
22 to *23:* 3 ws tw1   „   „   „   „   „
23 to *24:* 4 ws tw1   „   „   „   „   „
24 to *25:* 4 ws tw1, pin under wpr, tw1 wpr, ws tw1 wpr
through 2 prs and leave.

With pr from *18*, continue footing *6* as before: complete
triangle *6* to *11* before you can make next fan.

REMEMBER In order = 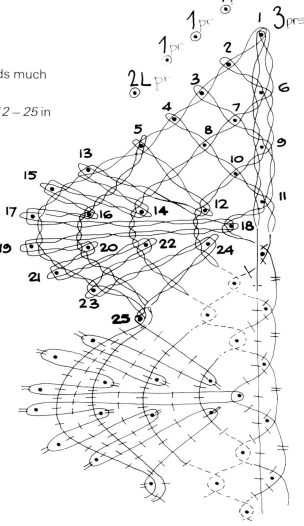 ; in pairs = ;

ws = ————— ; hs = – – – – – – –.

Handy hint: this type of twisted ws lace needs much
pulling/stroking to keep neat and tidy.

When going round a pin at edges of fans etc (*12 – 25* in
this pattern), THIS is a good habit to develop:

ws pin twist, separate
THREADS to make
twists settle round pin.

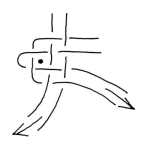

After next ws below pin – separate both
PAIRS to further guarantee the twists
are in the correct place.

3. Torchon fan (also called Fir-tree fan) (cont.)

8 prs – Brok 36
Introducing: Torchon ground; hanging on in pairs;
twisted ws fan

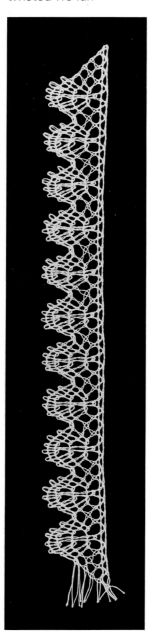

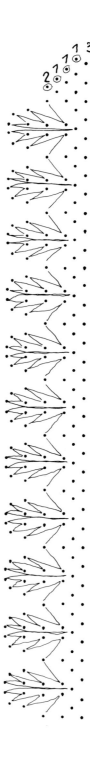

Setting up or moving your lace

There are times when you need to move your lace during working.

In the old days the poor lacemaker only had one pricking, called a 'down', measuring approx 40cm. When the lace reached the end of the pricking *all the pins* had to be removed, *all the work* moved back to the top and *all the pins* replaced for at least one repeat!! Very, very time-consuming and fraught with danger for the beginner. Nowadays we are much luckier with block pillows for corners and roller pillows for continuous work, but sometimes it is still necessary to move the work.

'Setting up'

First all tension must be removed from threads.
Use your worker cloth to parcel your bobbins.

1. Thread elastic or cord through all spangle loops and tie together (keeps bobbins in order).

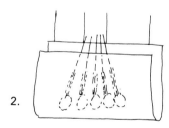

2. Fold bottom of worker cloth up over bobbins.

3. Fold sides in and pin through all layers of cloth.

Move this parcel up slightly, to remove tension from threads; pin to pillow.

Now you can *carefully* remove all the pins.

Move your lace and replace at least 5cm of pins, taking special care of gimps and foot-side passives, as these can pull up incredibly easily.

Felt mountains

A clever invention to reduce further the number of pins to be removed and replaced.

You will need two prickings for this method.

Cut felt into strips 5cm wide and 8, 7, 6, 5 and 4cm long.

Place them on top of each other and sew through all layers to create a mini-mountain.

TURN UPSIDE DOWN TO USE

Place mountain *under* pricking so finish ends up on the plateau.

Work down and on to the mountain (your pins are now more on felt than on pillow); parcel bobbins as before, remove pins not in mountain and carefully remove all to top of pillow.

Butt new pricking up to existing pricking, continue down the mountain and you are away again.

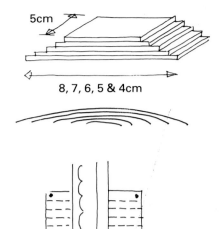

5cm

8, 7, 6, 5 & 4cm

Traditional pincushion

fold diagonally, right sides together

sew 2 sides – leaving small gap, turn inside out, stuff very full with bran or wool fleece, sew up gap

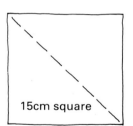

15cm square

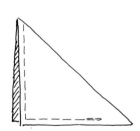

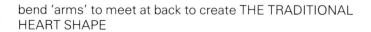

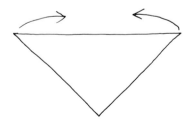

bend 'arms' to meet at back to create THE TRADITIONAL HEART SHAPE

pin to pillow through 'arms'

Bobbin carrier

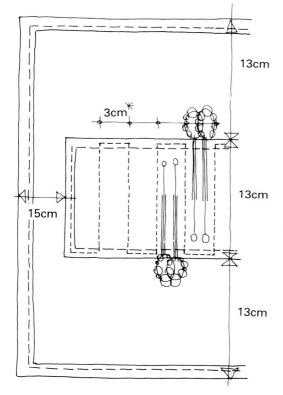

Can be made in any length

* size of compartments depends on size and type of bobbins – 3cm is perfect for a pair of normal beaded bobbins.

ALL SIZES GIVEN ARE *AFTER* HEMMING

13cm

3cm

15cm

13cm

13cm

when filled with prs of bobbins each side turn in flaps

and

roll up and tie with tape

4. 3D Flowers, the perfect gift

8 prs – Brok 36 + 1 pr thin fuse-wire gimp
Introducing: Gimps, adding-in and throwing-out

Wind approx 50cm thread on wpr only.

This pattern will be repeated at least five times and very little thread will be used on pprs, so wind plenty of thread on *one* bobbin per pr and just tie the thread onto the other. Then when one petal has been finished, all you do is pull off more thread from the full bobbin and tie again on to the other bobbin to make your new pr (saves valuable time and thread).

Use this method also for the wire gimp.

1. Hang on 4 prs *in pairs* on top petal-pin A. Make LH pair the wpr.

Gimps are usually a thicker outlining thread in all types of lace; in this case it is fine fuse wire to keep the petal shape.

> When a gimp is 'threaded through' always remember to lift up LH thread and pass gimp over RH thread – this applies whichever direction you are working.

The wpr is always twisted before and after passing a gimp through, to keep the gimp in position.

2. Hang gimp on ⊙ pin to left of work, take through all 4 prs, tw2 all 4 prs.

3. At *A* ws LH pr through next 3 prs, tw2, pass gimp through tw2, pin, take gimp through tw2.
    Remove ⊙.

> Gimp method at edges of this pattern:
> tw2 wpr, pass gimp through wpr, tw1, pin, pass gimp back again through wpr and tw2

4. 'Add-in' new pair, 1 pr from the end.

> Adding-in new pairs after start:
> New pr must always be 'hung-on' inside the outer prs of petal. This helps to keep the edges neat. A new pair is always added the row *before* the pin marked +1.

Hang new pair on a convenient ⊙ above; let it hang inside the outer pr.

5. ws through all 4 prs, tw2 etc.

6. work back and forth adding-in pairs each row until all 8 pairs are hung on.

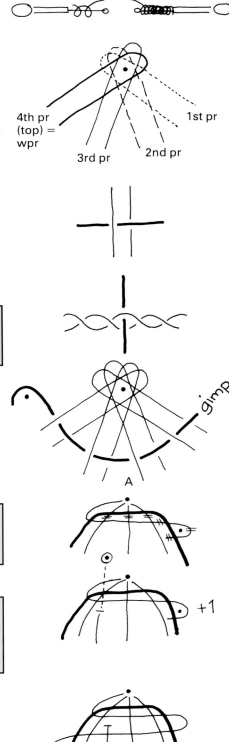

4th pr
(top) =
wpr

1st pr

3rd pr

2nd pr

gimp

A

+1

4. 3D Flowers, the perfect gift (cont.)

8 prs – Brok 36 + 1 pr thin fuse-wire gimp
Introducing: Gimps, adding-in and throwing-out

> The temporary pins must be removed after about 4 rows
> and threads *very carefully* pulled down to new position –
> TAKE CARE NOT TO CREATE HOLES AT THIS STAGE.
>
> It is very, very important to watch your work all the time.

7. Now work back and forth without adding pairs until 5
   pinholes from the end.

   Good handmade lace must be fine, even work:
   with these petals a good shape is more important than
   straight lines.

   It is too easy to add more pairs to get an even look, but
   more skilful and less machine-like with beautiful curving
   lines. It will take practice but will be more rewarding in the
   end.

Throwing out pairs This is an easy way to dispose of
unwanted pairs when work gets narrower.

8. Work until you reach first symbol –*1*, work that pin and
   *ws to other side, work edge as usual, then lift up 2nd pr
   from gimp on RH side and lay it to back of pillow, work
   across to other side, work edge as usual, then throw out
   2nd pr from gimp on LH side, repeat from * once.

9. After last bottom, pin, bind with wire from gimps round
   tail for about 5cm. Cut tail threads.
   Cut all 'thrown out' prs leaving about 3cm of thread.

Carefully remove all pins, now you can cut the 'thrown out'
threads close to the work – it is always safest to cut after
work has been released from pins.

Make 5 petals, then bind together with some wire and some
stamens in the middle.

The flowers can be made in hs, with veining down the middle
(see page 18) or in coloured threads.

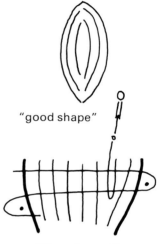

"good shape"

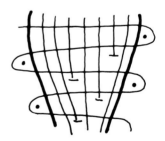

"throwing out"

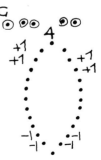

Pricking   47

General instructions for starting bookmarks

- Use 2 threads as one, hs pin hs at *1*.
  Work down LH side, again using pairs from *1* as single threads, work hs pin hs, tw2 RHPs.
  Repeat RH side but tw2 LHPs of course.
  NO EXTRA TWISTS AT *8* and *9*. This doubling up of edge prs looks better visually.

Remove all ⊙ .

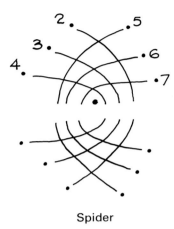

Spider

Spiders

ws pr from 2 through 3 prs to R
ws pr from 3 through 3 prs to R
ws pr from 4 through 3 prs to R

pin in middle

ws pr L of centre through 3 prs to R
ws next pr to L of centre through 3 prs to R (twice)

Tw3 all 6 prs (called legs).

Fans

Draw in rest of working lines of fans as shown.

If at the end of a fan the work looks slanted and you finish in the wrong place (e.g. pinholes *36* or *29*, YOU ARE WRONG! The worker must always end up on the outside of the valley pin.

Valley Pin = pin between two fans (e.g. *37*).

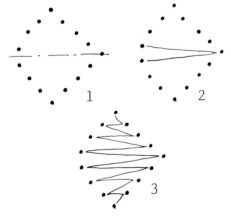

Drawing in fan lines

When two fans meet, work top half of one fan, hang wpr temporarily on a pin, work top half of other fan until same position, remove temporary pin, ws both wprs through each other, pin, ws through each other again, and now finish the fans.

N.B. When creating a fan, the final shape is very important – see diagram.

Aim for lovely curving lines

5. Daisy bookmark

12 prs – Brok 36/3
Introducing: fans and spiders
10 prs – 50cm; 2 prs – 150cm (per bobbin)

These bookmarks make ideal presents – play with colours next, then with textures and materials.

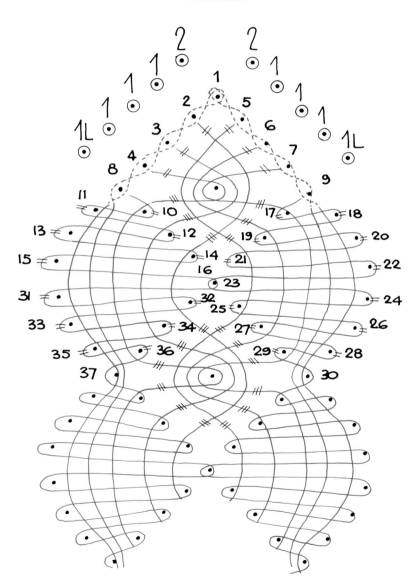

Finishing off

Discard wprs. Using 2 prs passives as one thread, hs pin hs with single threads from spiders.

At bottom hs pin hs using both sets of double threads.

There are many many ways to finish; most depend on personal taste – see page 82. I recommend at this stage you try the simplest:

Divide all the pairs into small equal groups; tie each group with an overhand knot. You will have more control over positioning the knot, if you put a long pin in the centre of the knot and guide the knot with the pin to its final place, before pulling the knot tight.

Overhand knot

5. Daisy bookmark (cont.)

12 prs – Brok 36/3
Introducing: fans and spiders
10 prs – 50cm; 2 prs – 150cm (per bobbin)

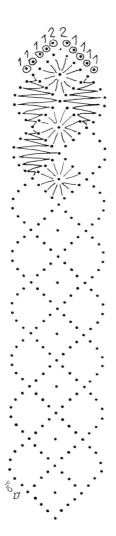

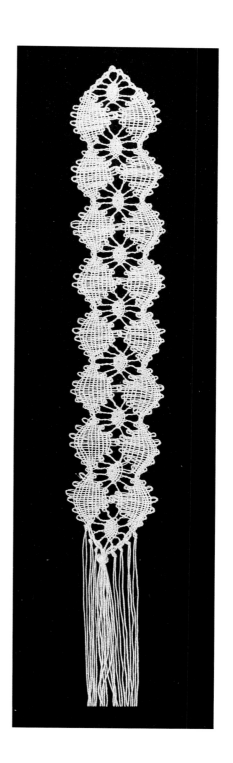

6. Love-in-a-mist bookmark

16 prs – Brok 36/3
Introducing: Brabant Ground

Start as Daisy Bookmark

hs pin hs throughout
diamond *1 – 20*

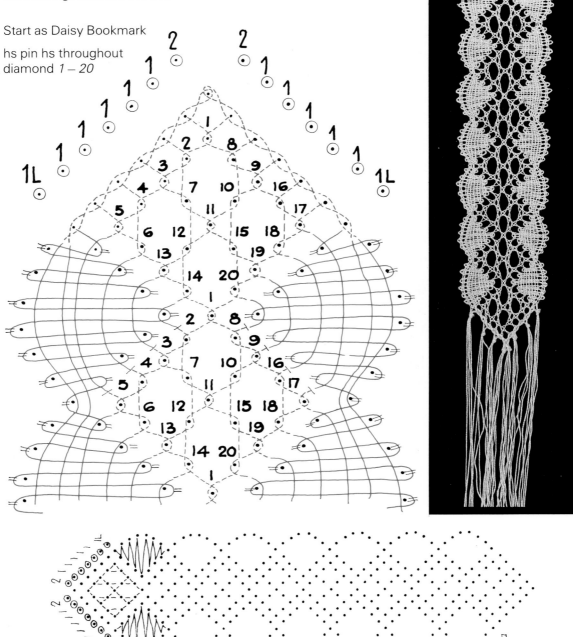

7. Lobelia bookmark

14 prs – Brok 36/3
Introducing: Rose Ground and mini-spiders

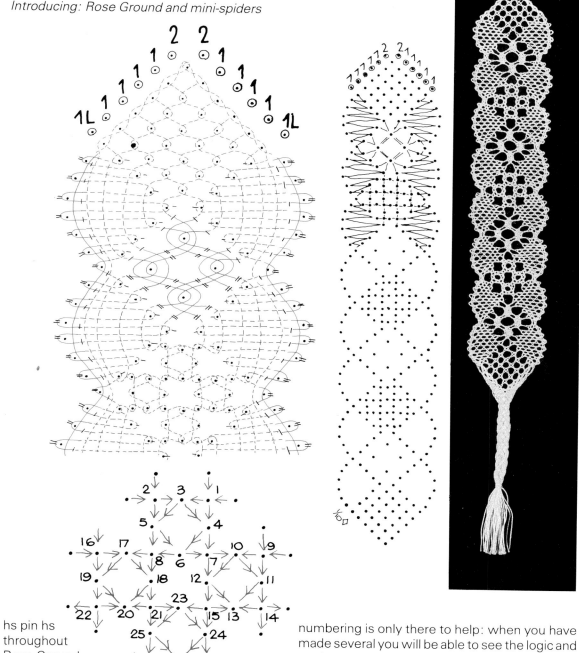

hs pin hs
throughout
Rose Ground

numbering is only there to help: when you have
made several you will be able to see the logic and
work out your own routine

8. Bluebells bookmark
— variations on a theme

12 prs – Brok 36/3

Make special note of
number of twists

ws with
twisted wpr

twist wpr
and pprs

tw1 wpr before
and after edge pr

hs with
ws edge

hs with
twisted
ws edge

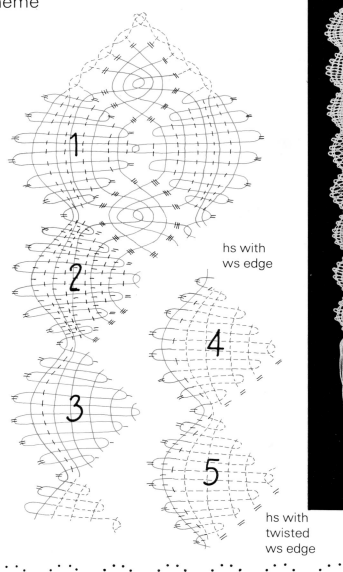

Spiders galore

Now you have mastered the standard spider, below are nine different versions to make you realize how many ways YOU have to personalize your lace — the deciding factors being the number of prs coming in and going out of the diamonds.

Top five have 6 legs; bottom four have 8 legs.

Add to this list when you find more — which you surely will!

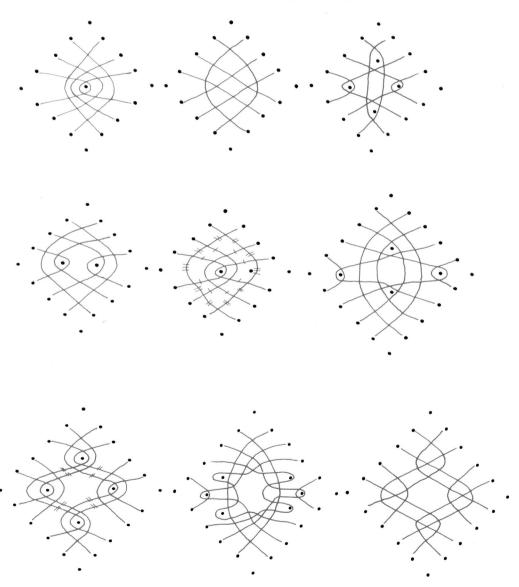

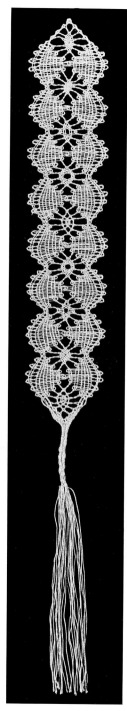

Six-pair crossings

I have come to the conclusion I shall never be able to remember multiple-pair crossings and equally cannot bear to write out endless words – so I have devised this code, easy and quick to note down.

WORK EACH PR AS ONE THROUGHOUT

∪ = under   ∩ = over   ∿→ = over/under L to R   R to L ←∿

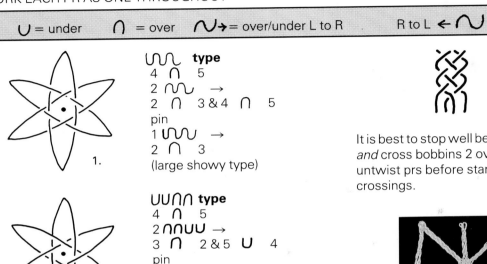

∪∪∿ type
4 ∩ 5
2 ∿ →
2 ∩ 3 & 4 ∩ 5
pin
1 ∪∪∪ →
2 ∩ 3
(large showy type)

1.

∪∪∩∩ type
4 ∩ 5
2 ∩∩∪∪ →
3 ∩ 2 & 5 ∪ 4
pin
1∪∪∩∩ →
2 ∩ 3
(tighter then above)

2.

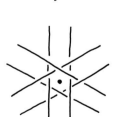

Quick type
hs 4 outer prs *over* centre prs
pin
2 ∩ 3 under centre prs
(loose but easy)

3.

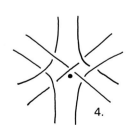

Triangular type
2 ∩ 3 & 4 ∩ 5
2 ∩ 1, & 4 ∩ 3 & 6 ∩ 5
pin
2 ∩ 3, & 4 ∩ 5
(decorative but . . .)

See also page 32 for 4 pr crossing; page 74 for 8 pr crossing.

The choice is *YOURS*.

4.

It is best to stop well before pinhole *and* cross bobbins 2 over 3 to untwist prs before starting crossings.

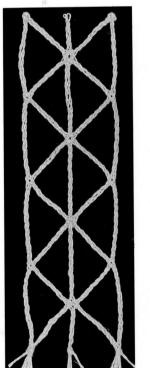

1.

2.

3.

4.

9. Modern Bedfordshire 'leaves'

2 prs – Brok 36/3

There is much controversy about these woven shapes. In the old 'Beds' laces they were blunt-ended and called tallies. They are difficult to get neat.

I feel lace must advance, so I prefer the idea of using a modern shape and calling it a LEAF

- To start, hang 2 prs over top pin, tw2 both. Braid (continuous hs) to next pin, pin between prs, *ws through each other*.

- For the leaves, elongate the thread that will be the weaver – no. 3 in this instance. Hold the weaver thread so no tension is on it whilst weaving; take weaver under 4 and pull *tight*.
  THE OBJECT IS TO GET A TIGHT START AND FINISH.

> * back over 4 under 2 over 1
> back under 1 over 2 under 4
> hold threads 1, 2 and 4 taut with one hand, and pull weaver to create desired shape*
>
> Repeat from * to * until bottom

- I like to knot the weaver with central thread so the leaf shape is not lost the moment you let go of the weaver thread.

- Pin between prs and braid to next pinhole; pin between prs, tw2 (this makes large hole for sewing together later), braid to next pinhole etc., etc.

Try to correct mishaps by pulling various individual threads, but if all else fails *unpick until it is right* – lopsided, too narrow or too wide leaves give character, but holly leaves are bad!

Handy hint: it helps enormously to have evenly matched bobbins (length and weight)

Use for sample – sew it onto a backing through these holes. Use this little exercise as a reminder before you embark on a pattern with leaves, rather like a pianist practises his scales. Try to lose the fear of leaves – you only achieve this with practice.

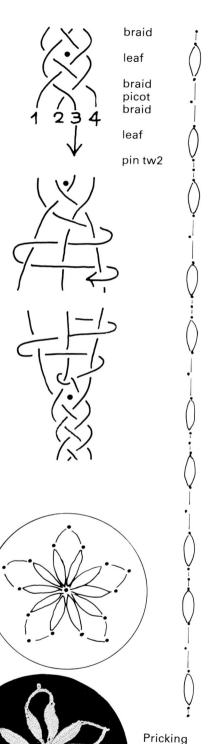

braid
leaf
braid
picot
braid
leaf
pin tw2

1 2 3 4

Pricking

Hook or needlepin sewings

Sewing is the method of joining sections of lace together, using either a very fine crochet hook (0.60) or a needlepin (fine needle stuck into a handle).

I strongly recommend you work with string to begin with – you will be able to experiment and understand WHY.

Using the method shown here the threads lie nice and flat; other ways work but not so neatly.

All sewings are shown as ⊡ on my prickings.

1. separate threads, remove pin

2. insert hook down from above, catch bottom thread

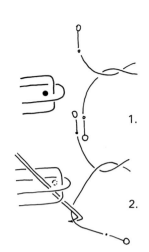

3. pull this thread through pinhole loop to form second loop; thread other bobbin through this loop

    replace pin

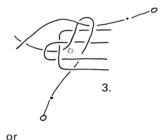

or

4. pull all tight, tw2

Handy hints: It is worth noting some distinguishing mark which shows which way up your hook is (I know when brand name is on top, the hook is down on my hook); this saves many abortive attempts.

Keep hook in loop while pulling tight after move 3 (helps stop the thread looping over all the wrong pins).

Remove pins while sewing: REPLACE PIN IMMEDIATELY AFTERWARDS.

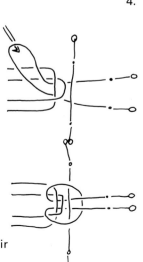

58

Sewing in more than one pair

Summary of modern pillow types and their uses

Size is very important — too large rather than too small is the rule.

Lacemaking takes long enough, so do not give yourself extra trouble because your bobbins are always falling off your small pillow.

All pillows must be firm, so pins do not wobble.

All must be covered with removable washable material — you will be amazed how dirty they get.

1. Basic beginner's pillow: see page 9.

2. Block pillow: see page 69.

   Ideal first 'real' pillow, good for continuous work, corners and circular work.

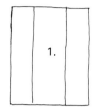
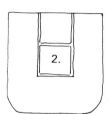

3. Roller type (modern French pillow): a miniature cylindrical pillow set into a desk.

   Very comfortable but of limited use — excellent for mileage work. They come in many shapes — oval, round and squarish, *but* make sure that:

   a. cylinder not set too high (my favourite is 4cm)
   b. there is enough room for bobbins to lie flat
   c. the slopes are not too steep
   d. the cylinder diameter is not too small

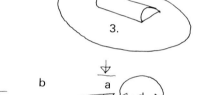
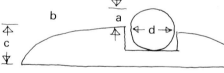

4. Mushroom-type pillow: see page 75.

   Very useful; ideal for Bedfordshire-type work and circular work, *but* make sure that:

   a. it is no smaller than 50cm diameter
   b. it is not too domed
   c. it has a gently curving, very firm surface.

   A 65cm diameter mushroom pillow is very useful for large projects, especially for tape and continental laces.

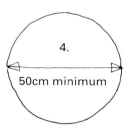

5. Honiton pillow: Honiton lace usually only consists of small individual items so you only need a very small pillow. Still, it must be firm and not too rounded. Watch out: there are some Honiton pillows that are *too* hard — you must be able to push pins right down into pillow without bending the pins.

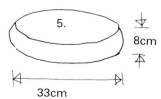

10. Ethel medallion

14 prs – Brok 36/3 and tiny elastic bands
Using 6 pr crossings, leaves and finishing off

At *A* work Lazy Join as page 32.

Braid from pinhole to pinhole as usual.

Picot where indicated – always on LH side throughout this pattern.

Add 2 new prs at *B*.

Hang 2 prs on ⊙ above *C*. Work Six-pair Cross at *C**. I wanted a tight crossing so I chose crossing No. 2 – see page 56. Remove ⊙ .

Work both braids to next pins before attempting the leaf.
* repeat at *D*, *E* and *F*.

Push all pins right down so you have plenty of space to make your leaf.

With this type of lace the pillow is turning so often that you have to work over pinheads occasionally. I am a great believer in using a transparent acetate thread protector (I save tops of sweet boxes). Fit it on pillow before starting and work through the centre hole.

CLEAR THE DECKS – remove all unnecessary pins and clutter, and move the pincushion out of the way (it will be moved often during this lace). It is all-important to have *space* while making your leaf.

Plan ahead so your finished work does not get in the way of work in progress.

Work round until all four leaves have been completed.

tw1 all 8 prs from *G*, *H*, *J*, and *K*.

pin between prs at bottom of *G*, hs through each other.

1 hs to *H**
4 hs to *K*
7 hs to *J*   7 hs to *L*   7 hs to *M*
4 hs to *N**
2 hs to *P*

(continued on page 62)

Adding-in prs at *C*, *D*, *E* and *F*

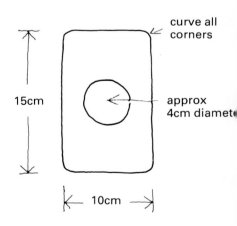

curve all corners

15cm

approx 4cm diamete

10cm

smooth, smooth edges essential throughout

10. Ethel medallion (cont.)

14 prs – Brok 36/3 and tiny elastic bands
Using 6 pr crossings, leaves, and finishing off

suitable for small picture or
paperweight

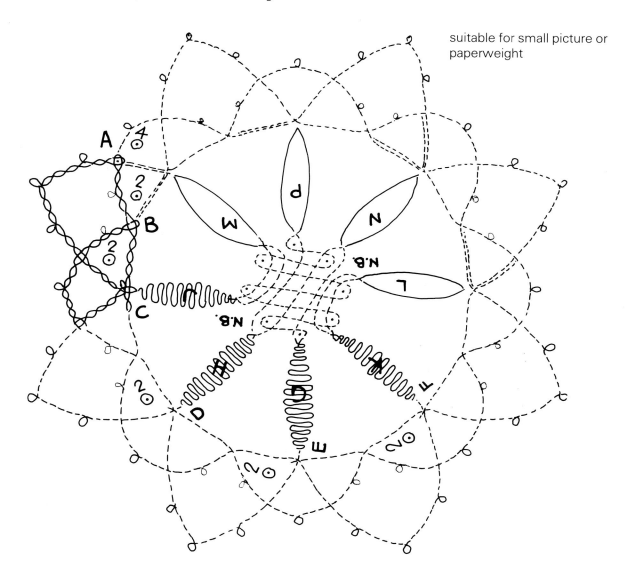

Handy hint: if your medallion is to be mounted in a frame,
sew with needle all the threads through original holes *and*
through backing and then knot.

* Picking up only one pr fills in the gap in hs circles that naturally occurs between H and J etc.

Work leaves *L, M, N,* and *P.*

Work 6 pr crossing where leaves join in braiding, double up any 2 internal threads with 2 threads that are leaving (use tiny elastic bands to help keep them together).

Work braids with extra care. Keep tight; after next join throw out unwanted threads; repeat again on other braid.

This is a marvellous, invisible way to lose unwanted pairs.

Continue round until end; sew threads through original holes, knot and cut off.

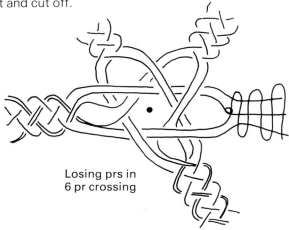

Losing prs in
6 pr crossing

Starting lines and finishing off

Starting

Obviously this is most important.

Find a place which will show the join the least e.g. the side of fans and diamonds are good places, also alongside gimps – easy to disguise.

Always start on the diagonal.

Corner starts are usually not ideal (weak point), except when there is a continuous hs trail – see Amanda Hanky, page 86.

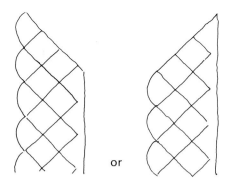

Starting lines

Completing your square/circle etc.

Replace all pins of first repeat then at least two more repeats of headside and footside.

If there is a gimp, it is essential to pin all round gimp for at least 3cm (can gather up at this stage).

Push ALL pins down until flush with pillow – this gives plenty of space to make that perfect join.

The whole aim is a strong invisible join:
PERFECTION WILL ONLY COME WITH PRACTICE.

- lengthen all *threads* until at least 20 cm long

- start at *footside*, remove pin and make sewing through original hole, reef knot plus – see diagram; leave this pair extra long (ready to sew onto fabric later), replace pin

  Sewing reminder (see page 58 for full details): separate threads, remove pin, insert hook, catch bottom thread, pull thread through pinhole loop to form second loop, thread through second loop, pull all tight

- remove *headside* pin, make sewing through original hole, reef knot, as above; leave this pair long also – ready to sew back behind fan or some solid feature, ws mass or gimps etc.

- sew *footside passive pairs* as above, weave back into passive pairs at end

- *the rest* – remove pin, sew, knot, replace pin and cut threads off leaving approx 5cm for the time being

- when all sewings completed carefully remove all pins except footside and headside pins; cut close the short ends, then release all from pins.

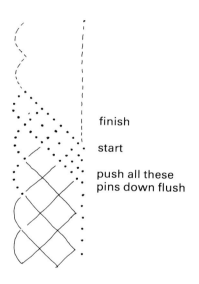

finish

start

push all these pins down flush

Finishing off

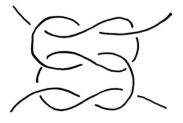

Reef knot plus

Turning a corner

Work until last diagonal line before corner.

NOW, VERY IMPORTANT: *turn your pillow* so you have a new vertical working line.

Start at top of outside fan.

You *must* start at the top and work down to the internal corner.

REMEMBER: NEVER WORK UPHILL. If you find too many pairs on one side of the work and not enough the other, you have committed the sin of working uphill (very easily done I might say).

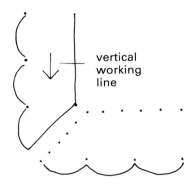

Corners generally

Corners are a fairly new invention in lacemaking.

In the old days lace was always made straight and then gathered round the corners. This can look very pretty. Patterns with a heavy headside and a lot of ground are ideal.

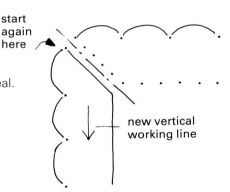

To *calculate how much lace* will take you round corners (it is always much more than you think), draw out accurately the finished hanky size; then measure round *external* circumference (all four sides!) plus a little more for shrinkage.

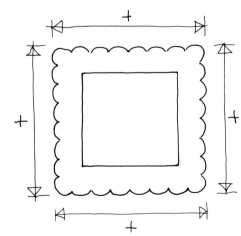

64

Designing corners

Very easy in Torchon lace

A clever way to find how your corner will look: use a mirror!

Hold mirror upright on any 45° line; move up or down finding the most satisfying solution; then draw along this line.

Match up with another 45° line going in opposite direction; cut half way between dots each side.

Match together: then hey presto – a new corner.

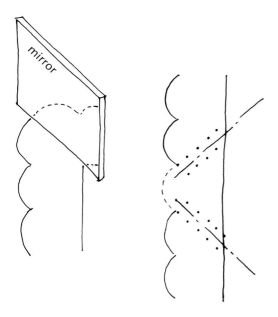

11. June hanky

14 prs — Brok 60
ws throughout
Introducing: corners and
finishing

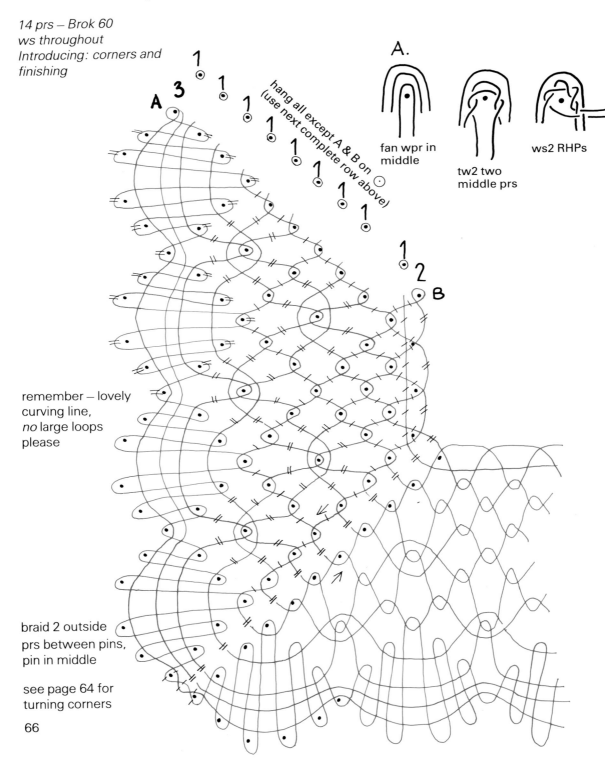

A 3

1
1
1
1
1
1
1
1

hang all except A & B on
(use next complete row above)

A.

fan wpr in
middle

tw2 two
middle prs

ws2 RHPs

1
2
B

remember — lovely
curving line,
no large loops
please

braid 2 outside
prs between pins,
pin in middle

see page 64 for
turning corners

66

11. June hanky (cont.)

14 prs – Brok 60
ws throughout
Introducing: corners and finishing

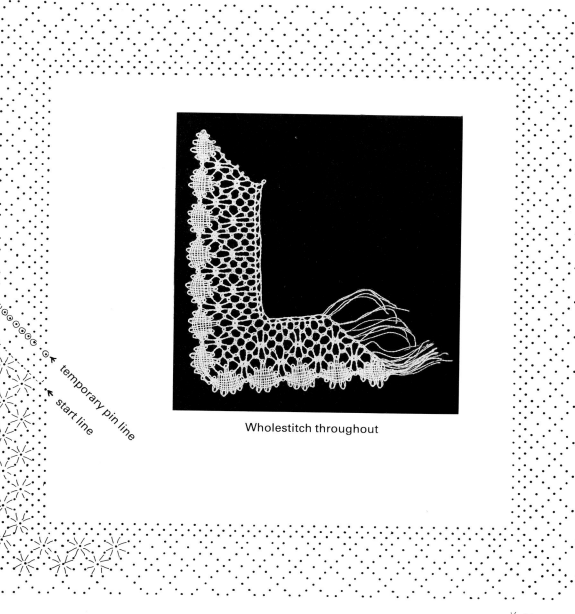

temporary pin line

start line

Wholestitch throughout

⅛ ☐

Finishing off your hanky

Make sure colour, texture and weight of material complement your lace.

Always press material before starting.

Cut material 4cm larger than hanky.

Draw out 2 or 3 threads on TWO SIDES of material roughly in position of join.

Pin, then tack lace to these 2 lines, so that footside just meets the drawn out thread line — starting from the corner each time.

Take care not to stretch either the lace or the material.

Only now draw out threads on next two sides to match lace, pin and tack.

Never be too impatient at this rather laborious start; it is so important and will repay you with a good finished article in the end.

Use a *tapestry needle* (this divides the threads rather than splitting them as ordinary needles) to sew lace to material. Try to use as thick a needle as possible to create those attractive holes we are aiming for.

Use lace footside pinholes as gauge for length of stitches.

Start with needle in front of work. Needle in at *A* and out at *B* (twice), back through *A* and out at *C* (diagonally across the back).

Take thread down in front and go in at *B* again which will be the new *A* for the next stitch; repeat round hanky, finishing off neatly at the back.

Now you have to cut excess material away.

Great, great care must be taken at this point, as I have found from bitter experience.

Remove tacking, fold lace back towards centre, one side at a time, then carefully cut as close as possible so that edge of material ends up under footside passives.

This raw edge can be oversewn, if subject to heavy wear, or left raw — the material has been oversewn many times already with this four-sided stitch.

Now you have a beautiful hanky.

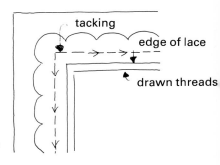

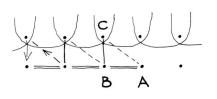

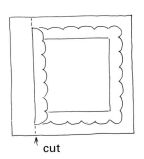

Block pillows

This is the most useful and adaptable pillow type.

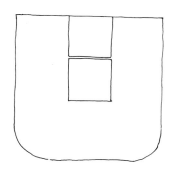

The two- or three-block pillow has square high-density (Styrofoam) blocks. You can work continuous lengths by shunting one after the other into the most comfortable working position.

It is worth investing in a circular insert for small circular work, and half-blocks for rectangular work.

It is essential to make sure the slope is not too steep (the bobbins will roll around too much if it is).

. . . . slope not too steep

Below are a few words of explanation that might help you to get the full benefit from this type of pillow.

It is essential to position your pricking correctly on the blocks, so that when a corner is turned the bobbins are still in a comfortable position.

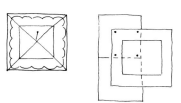

Find centre of pricking by drawing diagonal lines, put long pin in centre, find bottom RH corner of upper block with a long pin, then fasten and work top LH section first.

Dressing your block pillow

Again use plain, darkish blue or green smooth cotton material.

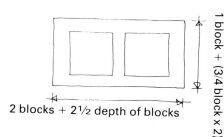

2 blocks + 2½ depth of blocks

1 block + (3/4 block x 2)

1. Blocks (pack out edges before covering to make firm fit, if necessary); make joins at edges to make tops reversible.

2. Pillow cover = pillow + 6cm: cut and turn fabric at edges, then glue with fabric glue at edges.

3. Worker cloth – half pillow + 4cm: hems sides and bottom. Use either selvedge or turn once and fix with Wonderweb or equivalent – very important that material does not rub your threads whilst working. I like to iron on a heavyweight interfacing to underside of this cloth (helps to smooth out bumps).

4. Overall cover cloth = 10cm larger than pillow and hemmed all round.

5. A nice finishing touch is narrow braid glued and pinned with brass drawing-pins.

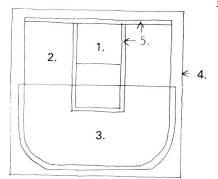

12. Torchon sampler
(Drawing-out exercise)

28 prs BOUC 30 (linen); 1 pr gimps –
BOUC 30 (4 strands) and 10cm wooden bar

You may find you have not enough bobbins
to make this pattern yet: never mind – still
draw out the exercise and make it later
when you have collected more bobbins.

In the meantime learn to 'read' diagrams
and prickings.

N.B. This is not the correct-size graph:
DO *NOT* TRY TO USE IT DIRECTLY

Draw out this pricking on ⅛" or 3mm graph
paper (see back of book). I recommend you draw
in pencil the various blocks and then fill in the dots
with pen and ink.

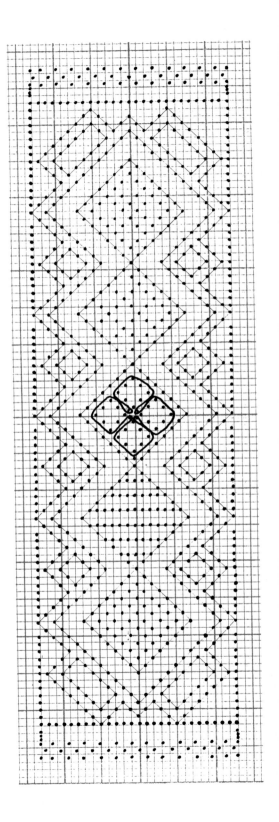

12. Torchon sampler (cont.)
(Drawing-out exercise)

28 prs BOUC 30 (linen); 1 pr gimps – BOUC 30 (4 strands)1
and 10cm wooden bar
Introducing: Bias, triangular and a new Rose Ground;
gimp work flowers

Fix bar to pillow

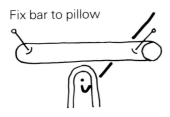

hang on bobbins as indicated
(N.B. wpr positions)

insert hook under bar and pull
pairs up

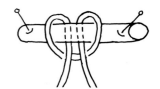

thread bobbins
through loop

tw1 between blocks throughout
internally except where shown
on diagram

tw2 both external edges

N.B. worker pr positions

A: hs block – no twists at pin;
   tw2 before and tw1 after

B: Bias Ground – hs or ws bars;
   note twist before and after

C: hs diamond tw1 round pin

D: Rose Ground
   hs pin hs 1 2 & 3
   hs 4 & 5
   hs pin hs 6 7 & 8

E: hs diamond tw2 round pin

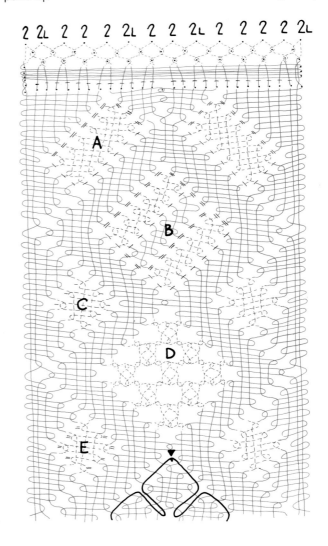

12. Torchon sampler (cont.)

Gimps (see note page 46)

Multiple strand gimp A technique often used in the past: it is sometimes difficult to find exact thickness and colour match, and this is the answer:

F: hang gimp on ☉
take gimp through (lift LH thread; pass gimp over RH thread) 3 prs to L and 3 prs to R, tw1 all 6 prs, ws top diamond, tw1 all 6 prs, take gimp through all 6 prs again, pass gimp round pin each side, tw1 all 6 prs *, return gimp back up through respective 3 prs and along next 3 prs waiting (see diagram), tw1, work next diamond

* usually when 2 gimps lie side by side, there are *no twists between* but I needed a gap, so tw1 this time

At end of flower – gimps are easy to finish off – just overlap well, twist well and throw out!! This time I have overlapped all 3 prs each side (less conspicuous), tw1 and continue as diagram; cut gimps close to work when they appear out of pins

G: hs diamond with extra twist to each passive every row

H: Triangular ground: ws throughout work in 3 diagonal rows, top centre down RH side first etc

J: hs diamond: tw1 round pin again

K: Tallies = square leaves: technique

basically same as page 57; you need plenty of space, so push all inconvenient pins right down. Torchon ground down both sides; work tally – good practice to *count* number of weaves, so all will look the same. Make slightly longer than square – will tighten up to become square later, tw1 both prs

Safe routine: work tally, secure weaver by working bottom RH pinhole first, the LH pinhole next, finally the bottom pinhole

L: hs block, wpr going in opposite direction to *A* (gives denser look)

AT END: pin between prs tw1, ws back and forth, hs pin hs, tie off with neat overhand knot – see page 50.

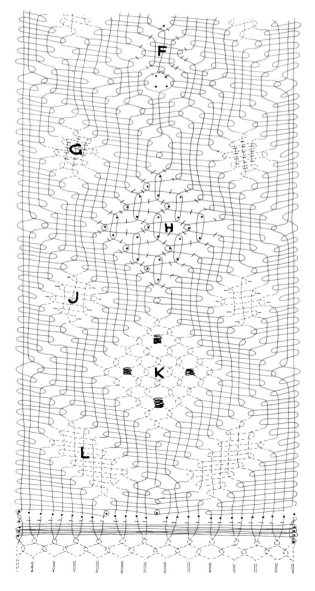

Eight-pair crossings

I have come to the conclusion I shall never be able to remember multiple-pair crossings, and equally I cannot bear to write out many words – so I have devised this code, easy and quick to note down.

Work each pr as one throughout

U = under	∩ = over	∿→ = over/under L to R

It is best to stop well before pinhole *and* cross bobbins 2 over 3 to untwist prs before starting crossings

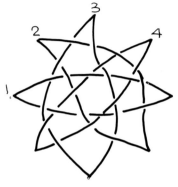

Popular type
hs centre 4 prs ⎫
hs RH 4 prs ⎬
hs LH 4 prs ⎭
Repeat
PIN
ws centre 4 prs
2 ∩ 3 and 6 ∩ 7

Decorative type
5 ∩ 4 and 7 ∩ 6
5 ∩ 6
2 ∿∿∿ →
5 ∿
5 ∩ 6
← ∿ ← 4
3 ∩ 4
PIN
1 ∿∿∿ →
3 ∩ 4
3 ∩ 2 and 5 ∩ 4

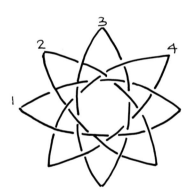

Quick type
hs prs from 2 and 4 over 3
ws both prs from 1 through
   all – L to R
lift up prs from 3
2 ∩ 3
replace prs from 3
   between prs 2 and 3

See also page 32 for 4 pr crossing
         page 56 for 6 pr crossing

The choice is *yours*

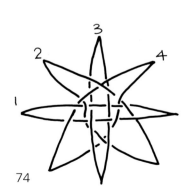

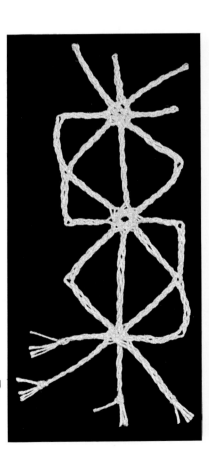

74

Mushroom-type pillow

A very useful pillow, ideal for Bedfordshire and circular work

To make it you will need:
50cm diameter 5 plywood   (a)

with 15cm-diameter hole in the middle   (b)

60cm diameter strong, non-stretchy material   (c)

(a) ⟶
(b) ⟶
(c) ⟶

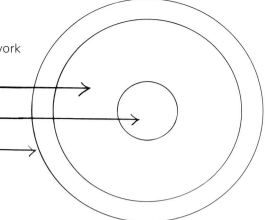

Construction

pleat and tack material to back of plywood ⟶

stuff with straw (preferably barley straw) through the hole in ⟶
the centre, starting at rim and moving inwards until no more
can be forced in — you will be amazed how much straw is
needed

hammer well throughout

replace ply centre

nail 48cm diameter hardboard cover over all, as the base ⟶

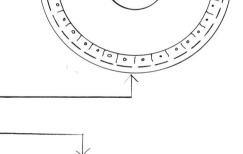

Aim for a gently curving, very firm surface. ⟶

straw

ply
hardboard

Make a removable cover with darkish blue or green plain
material, elasticated for easy removal for washing.

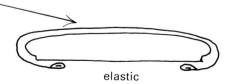

elastic

Handy hint: Mark centre of pillow with marker pen,
very useful when positioning your pricking.

13. Janice photograph frame sampler

14 prs – Brok 36 and 1 pr DMC Coton Perlé 8
Introducing: Various fillings and designing

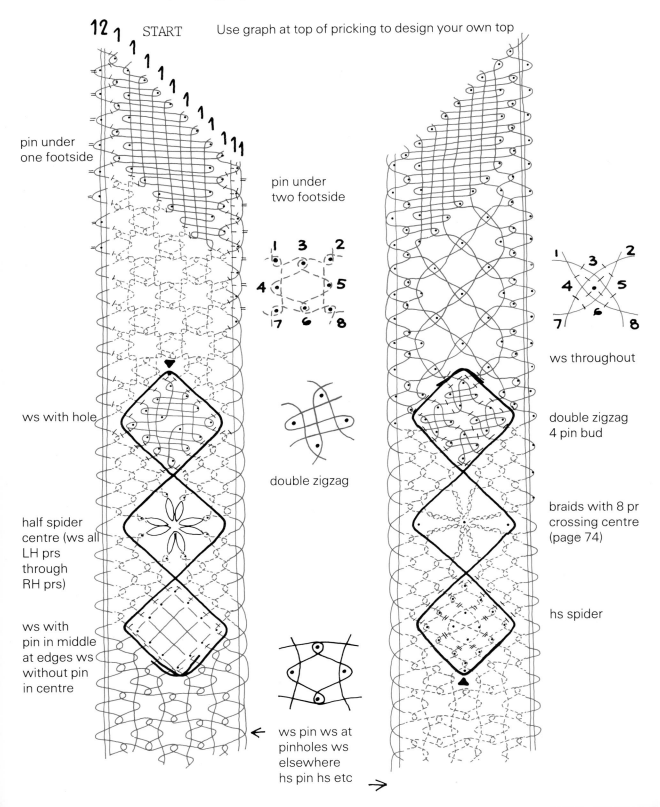

12 1 START   Use graph at top of pricking to design your own top

pin under
one footside

pin under
two footside

ws throughout

ws with hole

double zigzag
4 pin bud

half spider
centre (ws all
LH prs
through
RH prs)

braids with 8 pr
crossing centre
(page 74)

double zigzag

ws with
pin in middle
at edges ws
without pin
in centre

hs spider

ws pin ws at
pinholes ws
elsewhere
hs pin hs etc

13. Janice photograph frame sampler (cont.)

14 prs – Brok 36 and 1 pr DMC Coton Perlé 8
Introducing: Various fillings and designing

Remember to take gimp through, i.e. lift up LH thread, pop gimp through gap and over RH thread.

Hang gimp pr on ⊙ just above top pin; take gimp through all necessary prs to L and R; always make sure there are twists before and after gimps.

If in doubt about number of twists refer to photo of sampler.

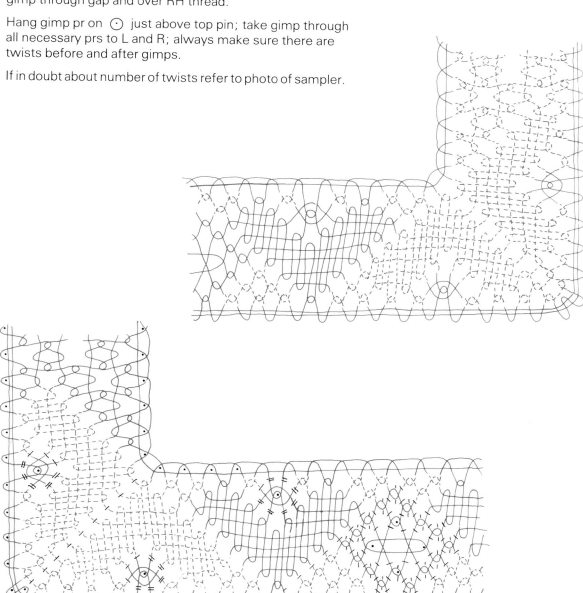

Rescuing a disaster

When making large projects using more thread than can comfortably be wound onto the bobbins, deliberately wind different lengths, so they do not run out all at once, making a very weak patch in your lace.

Special wholestitch

If your wpr is running out you must exchange it for a ppr first. There are various methods to use to exchange your prs; always choose places least visible – usually in ws passives or near gimpwork. Special wholestitches: by giving an extra twist to stitch round pin you can exchange wpr for ppr and with care it will never show.

SPECIAL WHOLESTITCH

extra 2 over 3 at end (bottom wpr swaps with outside ppr)

extra 2 over 1

extra 4 over 3

extra 2 over 3 at start

Adding-in new threads

Tie new thread to a pin. Ideal in ws areas; pin new thread to back or side of pricking, bring thread down by the side of thread to be replaced, join the two bobbins together with a tiny elastic band and use them as one for about 2cm, remove rubber band and throw out old thread.

Throwing out

Means placing the reject bobbin and thread to top of work, carefully cut off after another 5cm of work.

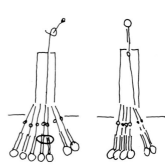

Adding-In   Throwing-Out

Magic knot (weaver's knot, lacemaker's knot)
When a disaster happens and a thread breaks, use this knot to join the threads. The knotted thread must be removed by above methods. KNOTS ARE NEVER ALLOWED.

1. make slip knot

leave this loop *large* as well

leave long

broken thread from work

2. loop broken thread through 'lassoo'

3. hold or get a friend to hold *onto* pillow this loose end until last minute – just before thread 'pops' through

Gently pull apart ends of new thread until old thread 'pops' through new loops. Experiment with string: you will feel there is a definite click as this happens

trim

4. knot looks like this before being pulled tight
trim off excess thread

Bookmark tops and tails

When you start designing your own, you will find useful this range of basic starts and finishings.

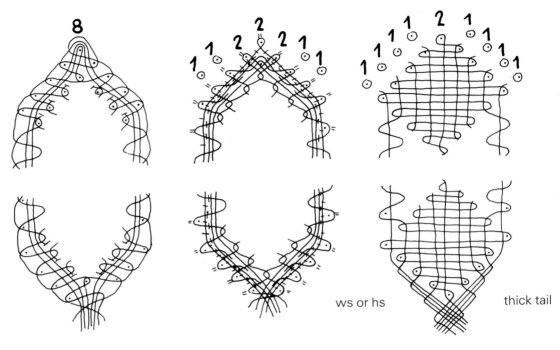

ws or hs

thick tail

Pin-under-two edging.
Adding-in internally
(see page 88).

Mock picot & twisted edge.
Adding-in in passives (invisible).

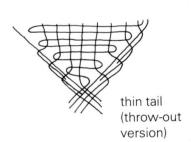

thin tail
(throw-out
version)

82

 LHP round ⊙ over pprs under RHP

 RHP under pprs through LHP remove ⊙ pull neat

 RHP round ⊙ over pprs under LHP

 LHP under pprs through RHP remove ⊙ pull neat

Repeat these four steps until required length

Macrame tail

 * tw1 LHP, ws to R tw1 *; repeat * to * pulling tight each row — can also be made in hs

Plait tail

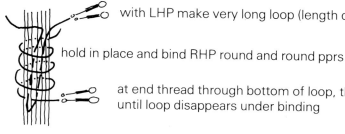 with LHP make very long loop (length of binding plus)

hold in place and bind RHP round and round pprs

at end thread through bottom of loop, then gently pull LHP until loop disappears under binding

Whipped tail

14. Running river

20 prs — Brok 36
Introducing: Bedfordshire trails, and Changing Workers;
best made on mushroom pillow

Hang on prs as shown (no definite wprs in Beds Lace, please note)
WS *A* to *B*.

Lazy join 4 prs from ⊙'s above *C*. Pull down to *C*.

Braid to *D* and *F*, ws *B* to *D* picking up braid prs from *C*, remove ⊙ above *B*, gently pull down to *B*. Pin braid prs out of the way (so you do not accidentally take back into trail).

Ws to *G* again pin. Braid prs out of way.

Add 2 new prs above *F* with lazy join. Braid to *H* and *L*.

Ws back and forth picking up braid prs at *H*.

Ws back and forth to *J* — pin braid prs out of way at *J*.

Form Ninepin Lace with 2 prs from *K* and 2 prs from *F* (see page 32).

Ws and Ninepin to *M*.

Braid and picot from *B* to *P*; leave (picots always on *left* in this pattern).

Work footside as usual with 4 prs until *P*.

Take in braid prs at *P*, pin and leave out again, continue footside until double bars *Q*, tw2, pin and leave.

Braid and picot from *P* to flower centre.

Braid prs from *E* and *J* to flower centre.

Flower centre

Pin between prs from *E* at top of flower, work hs taking in braids on either side

At = CHANGE WORKERS, that is tw1 pin under flower wpr,
  ws with wpr from footside, tw2 both.

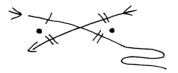

Continue flower with new wpr, change workers again on LH side at *M*.

Leave out 2 prs at *R S* and *T*. Braid as indicated.

Work Ninepin and ws river, taking in and leaving out as pattern dictates; remember braids from *S* and *T*. Stop at *U*.

Work footside from = until braid from *R*, take in, pin and leave out.

Continue footside until next =.

At *U* take in braid plus picot and leave wpr at =.

After change of workers pattern starts again.

Take great care with passives at bottom of curves — it really is a very tight fit; so much more stroking/pulling is necessary to get a smooth, even 'river'.

14. Running river (cont.)

20 prs – Brok 36
Introducing: Bedfordshire trails, and Changing Workers;
best made on mushroom pillow

This old Bedfordshire pattern is meant to represent the
meandering River Ouse at Bedford, with the many waterlilies
that lie on the river there.

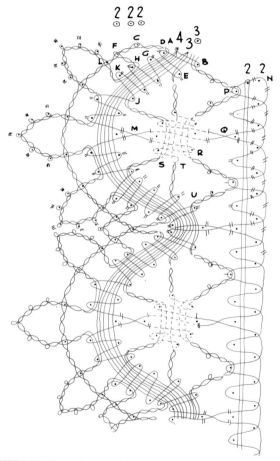

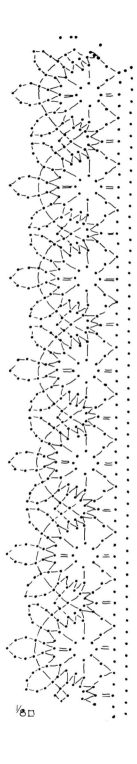

15. Amanda hanky

15 prs – Brok 60 or Linen 120/2
Introducing: hs trails

Fans as Torchon Fan (page 40) but with more pprs

At * hs, pin hs then pin again, on next row, in front of wpr.
This method prevents normal thick-and-thin-look trail.

I suggest you draw in rest of trail lines before you start.

start line

16. French fan lavender bag

7 prs — sewing cotton 40
Introducing: Colour and French Fan

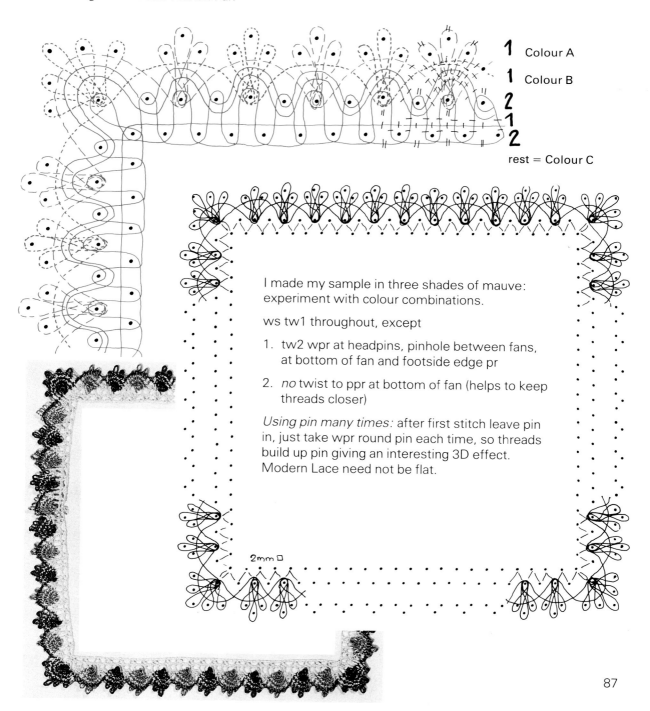

1 Colour A

1 Colour B

2

1

2

rest = Colour C

I made my sample in three shades of mauve: experiment with colour combinations.

ws tw1 throughout, except

1. *tw2* wpr at headpins, pinhole between fans, at bottom of fan and footside edge pr

2. *no* twist to ppr at bottom of fan (helps to keep threads closer)

Using pin many times: after first stitch leave pin in, just take wpr round pin each time, so threads build up pin giving an interesting 3D effect. Modern Lace need not be flat.

2mm ▫

Square starts There are three basic types

Read this page in conjunction with pages 114 and 115

1. Pin-under-one type

Hang two pairs on each pinhole, tw1 both, take horizontal pprs through (see note below).

2. Pin-under-two type

Start LH side. Hang 4 prs on A (in order); ws 2 LHP's, tw all 4 prs, hang 2 new pairs on next ⊙ to R (*B*)
* ws RHP through new LHP from ⊙, pin between these prs, remove ⊙ tw all 3 prs *

repeat from * to * until all prs taken in

Number of twists depends on pattern and thickness of thread to be used.

> *Hanging on pairs horizontally* Pairs must be anchored until work has progressed a little. Tie prs to pin; push pin firmly down into pillow to L of work, so LHPs do not move whilst working RHPs

3. Hanging on internally

Fix wpr and ppr to pillow to left of work as above, turn work so you work vertically, ws back and forwards adding in one or two prs as pattern demands.

(a) hang new pr on ⊙ above; ws through new pr from ⊙, pin between ws's then through new pr again

(b) pin under wpr, hang new pr on same pin tw1 wpr, ws through new pr tw1

(c) pin under wpr, hang 2 new prs on same pin, ws wpr through 1 pr tw1 wpr, ws wpr through next pr

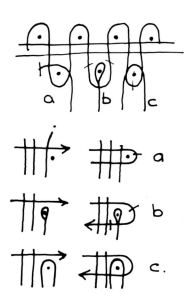

Square finishings

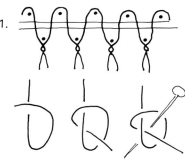

To be read in conjunction with pages 114 and 115
1. Fringe ending:
   Tie prs off with overhand knot: Easiest and very effective
   end for the right occasion.

For overhand knot, see page 50.

2. To match Pin-under-one-type top, the more pprs the
   easier to disguise the ending. 3 ws then throw out.

3. Pin-under-two type:
   I like to knot round pin on last row of general ground, for
   safety; then ws through 3 prs and throw out.

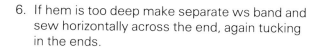

4. Good-solid-look end:
   tw1 before taking through 3 prs, then throw out.

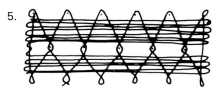

sew

5. Firm 'LACE HEM' top and bottom, to give strength
   to insertion lace in tablecloths etc. Good neat solution
   for hiding those ends, when the lace is subject to
   hard wear.

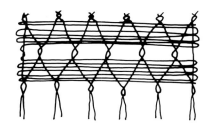

6. If hem is too deep make separate ws band and
   sew horizontally across the end, again tucking
   in the ends.

General rule on throwing out

Any pr to be thrown out either should be knotted
or should have been worked through at least 2 prs,
preferably 3 prs, before being thrown out.

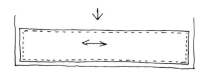

17. Linette mobile

16 prs — Brok 36, 15cm lampshade ring and 32mm curtain ring

This pattern offers an invaluable lesson in *planning ahead* with your work routine, to save unnecessary bobbin movement.

Firmly fix your rings to pillow with berry pins, BEFORE you start.

⊡ = Normal single sewing
ss = Double sewing (using 2 threads as one) on all braid sewings

I prefer to knot after both types of sewings round rings to keep all tight.

Work in sequence shown

Very important to start at *A* – see Starting diagram. To get overlapping correct, use Normal Working Sequence diagram.

Four-pearl filling is difficult to keep tight so follow sequence shown at *B*. Use thick pins to make large loops (see *The Book of Bobbin Lace Stitches*).

Take care going round bends!! Extra stroking/pulling will be needed to get all super-tight.

At *C* work through 5 prs, pin under two * leave wpr, work back to outer edge with next ppr, work pin under one edge*

work back through 4 prs, pin under 2, work * to *
work back through 3 prs, pin under 2, work * to *
sew at edge

Work as above in reverse order until all prs are back in work.

17. Linette mobile (cont.)

16 prs – Brok 36, 15cm lampshade ring and 32mm curtain ring

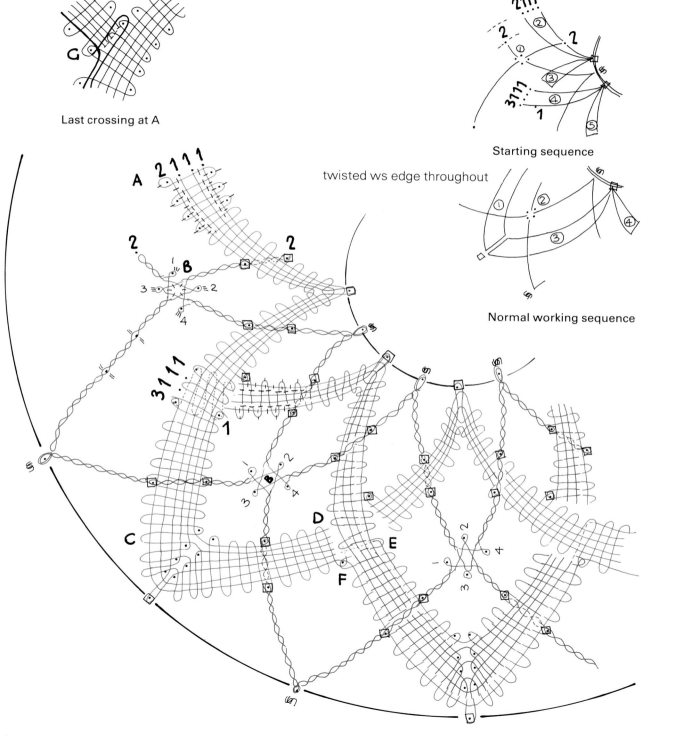

Last crossing at A

Starting sequence

twisted ws edge throughout

Normal working sequence

Overlap crossings

To achieve the thick-and-thin effect, 2 extra prs stay in the thicker parts, and are transferred at the crossings.

When *using pin twice* (e.g. *D*), carefully remove existing pin, work new stitch and replace pin in the same hole.

Leave out 1 pr at *E* and *F*.

Last crossing (*A*) (slightly different from other crossings).

Leave out pr at *G*. Sew out middle 5 prs, leave wpr.

These 2 prs will be worked into last arc.

At end: sew back into beginning, then tuck ends between layers to give that invisible finish.

Handy hints: Park your crochet hook under your pricking and hoop, between pins, when not in use — less likely to get lost.

I was recently introduced to a marvellous knitting gadget, ideal for confining your bobbins *in order* when not in use, called a Spring Stitch Holder. Just thread needle through bead loops, attach spring, then all is secure — invaluable for this pattern.

17. Linette mobile (cont.)

16 prs – Brok 36, 15cm lampshade ring and 32mm curtain ring

Picot survey

Practise with string and large pins to understand each technique fully.

No tension on picot threads throughout working

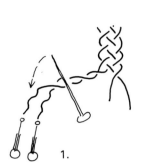

1.

Basic picot

2. and 3.

4. and 5.

Basic Picot – see p. 34

1. tw3, pin on top

2. twist threads round pin

3. put in pin

4. separate threads (to settle twists round pin)

5. tw1, continue braiding

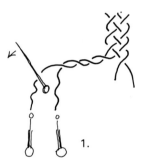

1.

tw3 (at least)

1. pin on top of outside thread

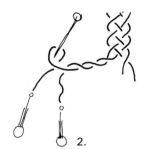

2.

2. twist pin downwards so thread loops round pin, put in pin

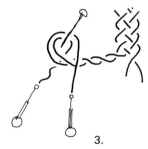

3.

3. hold outside thread to remove tension, twist other thread round pin in clockwise motion

4. tw2, continue braiding

Standard picot

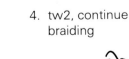

RH picots as LH except pin *under* and other thread round in *anti*-clockwise motion

Double picots: work picot, hs, work next picot

94

Knotted picot (for thick threads)

4.

1. hold pin in LH pin under and over threads

2. twist pin round

3. twist pin over vertical thread & back up through loop

4. pull knotted loop to size and pin

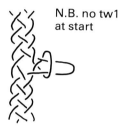

N.B. no tw1 at start

LH picot   RH picot

18. **Bells** for all occasions – weddings, Christmas, celebrations. . .

28 prs for each bell

Choose your size, then make a little sample before winding all the bobbins. Make as many bells as time allows, and attach them to veils, handkerchieves etc. for, that special occasion:

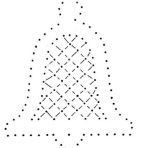

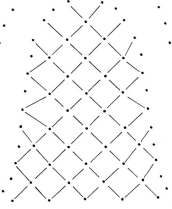

Brok 60
(size of sample)

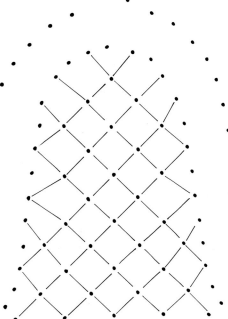

Barbour Linen 50

18. Bells for all occasions (cont.)

28 prs for each bell

Twisted ws edge throughout

N.B. for clever method of
adding pairs — just
follow diagram

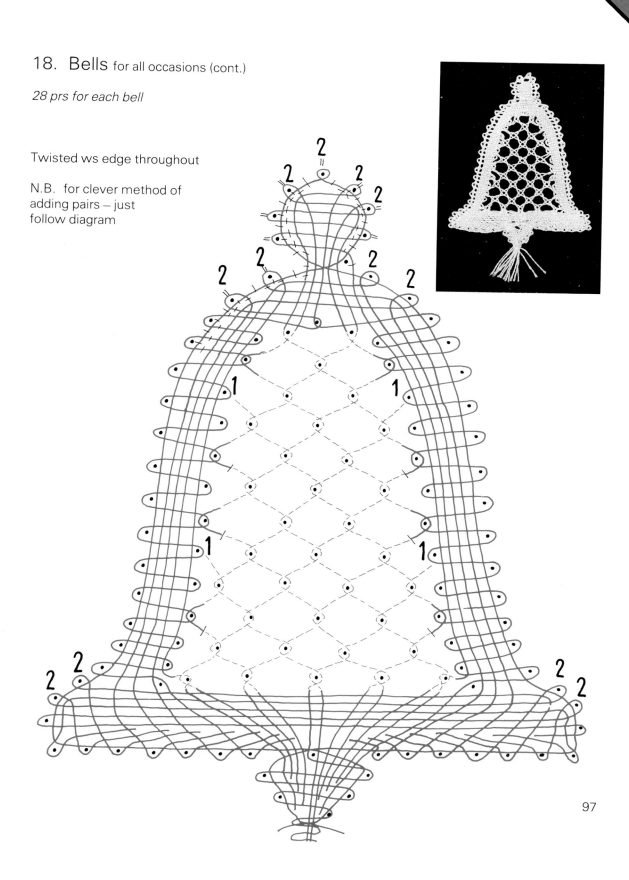

Trail crossings

When two trails cross in Torchon lace, there are several choices depending on pricking and whether you require a solid centre or a decorative hole.

Diamond centred

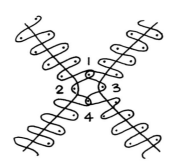

pretty Rose Ground effect (single pprs)

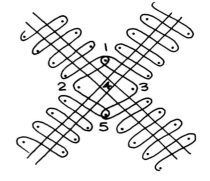

two + passive pairs

Continuous line type

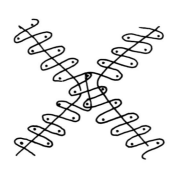

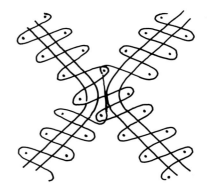

Miscellaneous types

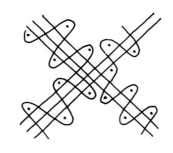

19. Crossroads

16 prs – Brok 36

Crossing trails and unusual spiders

For Spiders see page 55, for trails see opposite, for finishing and plaited tail see page 83.

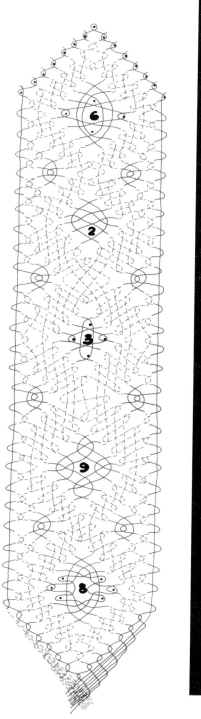

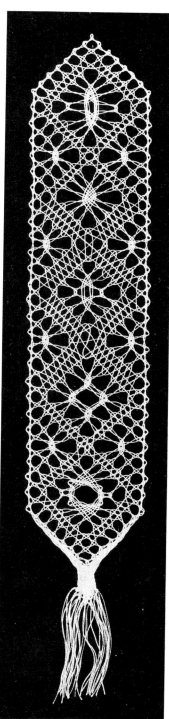

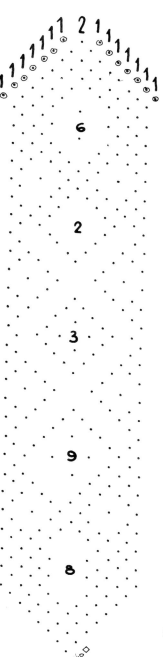

99

20. Table setting – Napkin Corner

30 prs – Bockens 50/2; 2 prs gimp – double-thickness Bockens 18/3

For pricking, see page 104; for photo, see page 107.

add 1 pr each internal pinhole down this side until widest point

Ground throughout: hs pin hs tw1 except near gimps – no extra twists

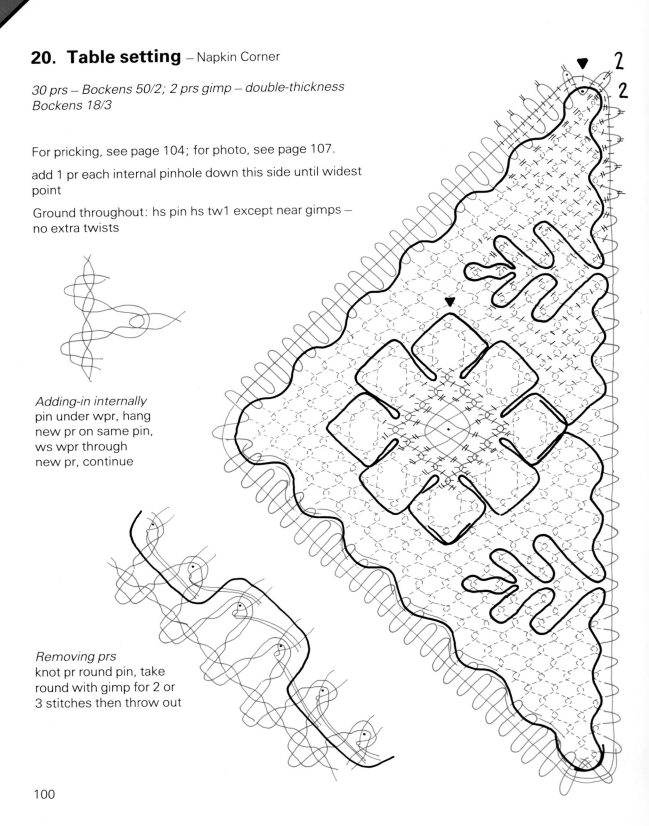

Adding-in internally
pin under wpr, hang
new pr on same pin,
ws wpr through
new pr, continue

Removing prs
knot pr round pin, take
round with gimp for 2 or
3 stitches then throw out

21. **Table setting** – Glass coasters

38 prs – Bockens 50/2; 2 prs gimp – double-thickness Bockens 18/3

Working straight down uses many prs but is much easier to finish.

Ground throughout: hs pin hs tw1, except near gimps – no extra twists

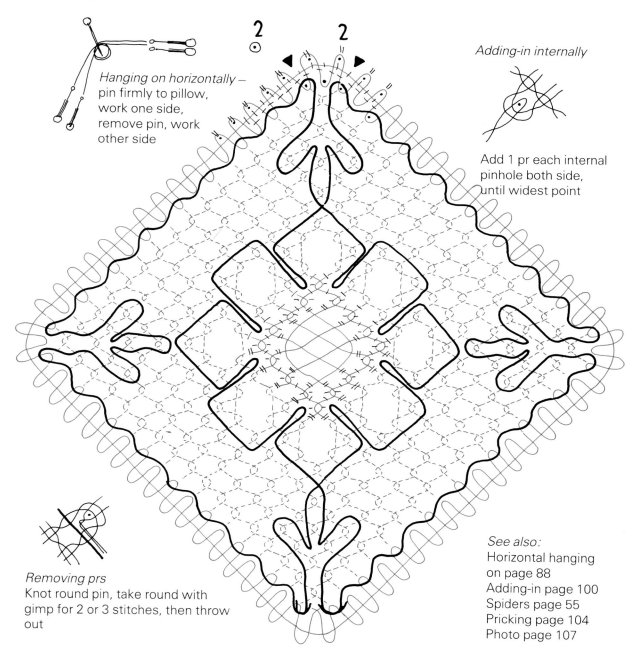

Hanging on horizontally – pin firmly to pillow, work one side, remove pin, work other side

Adding-in internally

Add 1 pr each internal pinhole both side, until widest point

Removing prs
Knot round pin, take round with gimp for 2 or 3 stitches, then throw out

See also:
Horizontal hanging on page 88
Adding-in page 100
Spiders page 55
Pricking page 104
Photo page 107

22. **Table setting** – Placemat edge

28 prs – Bockens 50/2; 2½ pairs gimp – double-thickness Bockens 18/3

Ground throughout: hs pin hs tw1, except near gimps – no extra twists.

See page 100 for adding-in method.

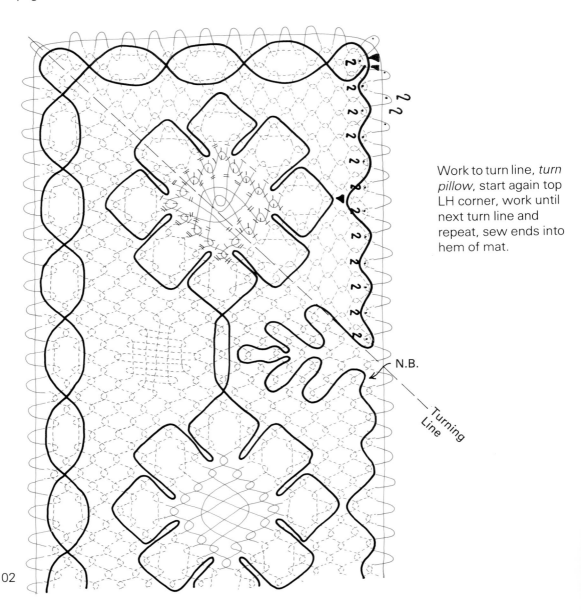

Work to turn line, *turn pillow*, start again top LH corner, work until next turn line and repeat, sew ends into hem of mat.

N.B.

Turning Line

23. Table setting — Tablecloth edging

*28 prs — Bockens 50/2; 2½ prs gimp — double-thickness
Bockens 18/3*

Ground throughout: hs pin hs tw1, except near gimps — no
extra twists.

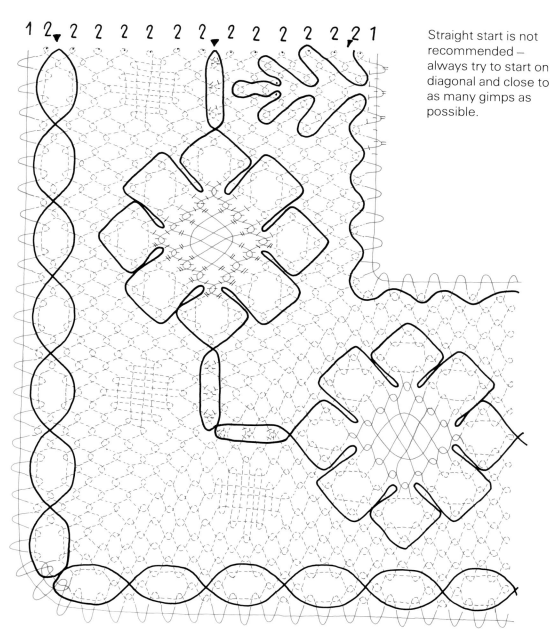

Straight start is not
recommended —
always try to start on
diagonal and close to
as many gimps as
possible.

Corner and coaster prickings (20 and 21)

*Bockens Linen 50/2 and Bockens Linen Gimp double
thickness 18/3*

Placemat edge pricking (22)

28 prs – Bockens 50/2 and 2½ prs gimp – Bockens double-thickness 18/3

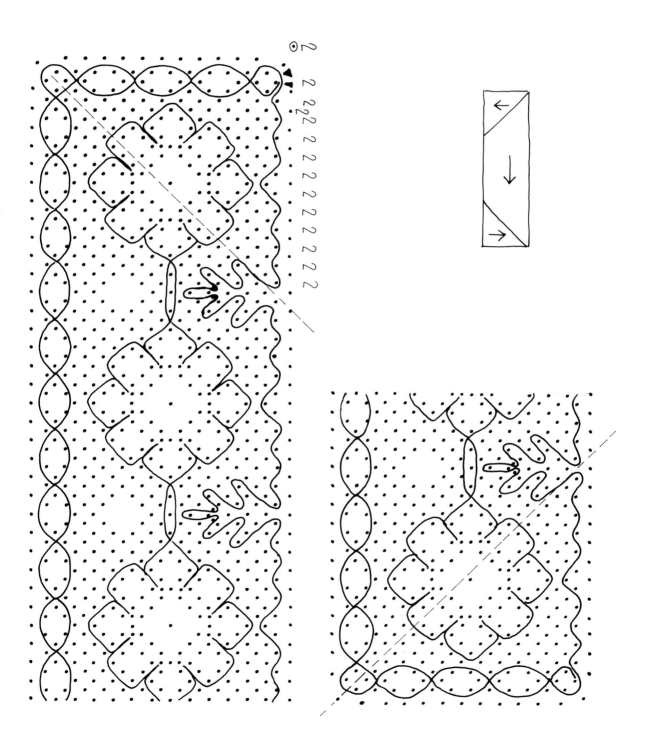

23 and 24. Table setting — Cloth edging and insertion

Bockens 50/2 and Bockens 18/3

See page 103 for numbers of bobbins.

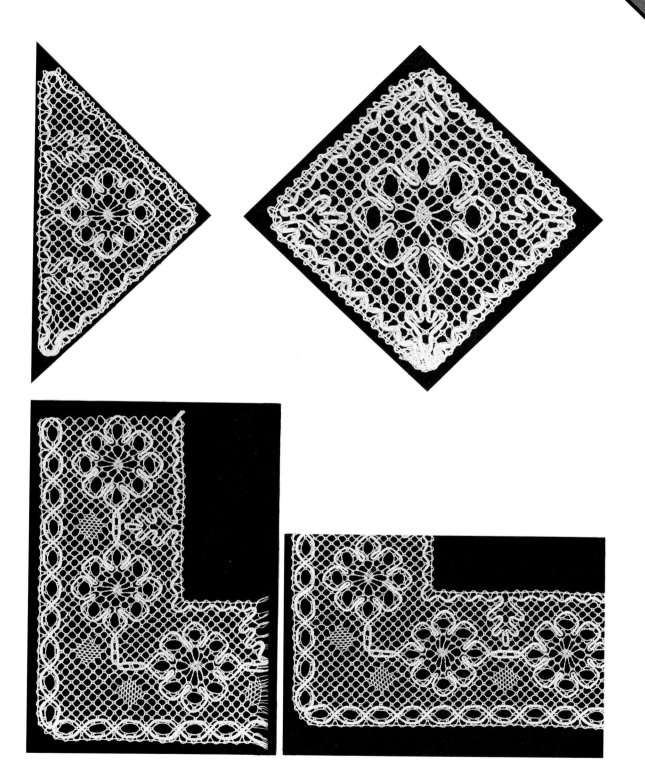

Identifying four typical English laces

English laces always have footside on the RIGHT

Typical Bedfordshire Lace has a spikey look
Threads – fine to coarse
Gimps – rare
Continuous lace
No set grid for prickings

LOOK FOR:

1. Ninepin edging – very common

2. Blunt-edged leaves for typical Old Bedfordshire

3. Braided bars between motifs, sometimes with picots

4. Raised tallies

5. Flowing thick and thin trails

Similar to Maltese and Le Puy Laces

See pages 57 and 84 for typical modern examples

Further reading:
Pam Robinson, *A Manual of Bedfordshire Lace* (Bean)
Margaret Turner, *Bedfordshire Lace Patterns* (Bean)

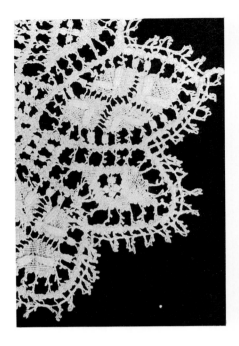

Typical Torchon Lace has a strong serviceable geometric look
Torchon is a French word for 'dishcloth' – presumably implying it washes well!
Threads – varies with countries and use
Gimps – sometimes
Continuous lace

LOOK FOR:

1. 45° grid

2. Torchon ground (hs pin hs)

3. Spiders, fans and diamonds – all very geometric

4. Headside either straight or fanned, never with picots

5. Very thick gimps usually indicate Scandinavian origins

Made throughout lacemaking world

Further reading:
Pamela Nottingham, *Technique of Bobbin Lace* (Batsford)
Pamela Nottingham, *Technique of Torchon Lace* (Batsford)
Jenny Fisher, *Torchon Lace for Today* (Dryad)

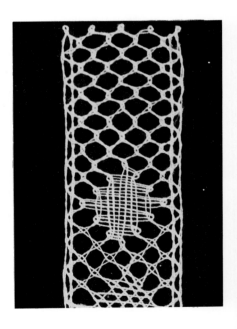

Typical *Bucks Point Lace* (a twisted net lace) has a fine
dainty lacey look
Threads — fine to very fine
Gimps — thick and shiny
Continuous lace

LOOK FOR:

1. 'Net look, a hs net stitch called point ground stitch — the
   most recognisable stitch

2. Gimp outlines

3. Honeycomb fillings — second most used stitch

4. Picots at headsides

5. Diamonds on their side in the net and on the prickings

6. Worked on a grid — varying from 45° to 60°

Similar to Lille, Chantilly & Tønder Laces

Further reading:
Geraldine Stott, *Visual Introduction to Bucks Point Lace*
(Batsford)
Pamela Nottingham, *Bucks Point Lace Making* (Batsford)
Geraldine Stott and Bridget Cook, *100 Traditional Bobbin
Lace Patterns* (Batsford)

Identifying four typical English laces (cont.)

Typical Honiton (Devon) Lace made throughout East Devon

Individual motifs sometimes sewn onto machine net to make large items such as wedding veils
Threads — fine to very fine
Gimps — yes
Non-continuous

LOOK FOR:

1. Individual motifs — thistle, shamrock and rose on this sample typical of Victorian era

2. Bars (brides) more common than net

3. Raised work, more difficult to work, therefore sign of better-class work

4. Gimp edging

5. Many sewings e.g. this little leaf: ws up one side then hs down the other sewing at each meeting point

Techniques similar to Brussels and Bruges laces

All made on a small circular pillow using small thin, *beadless* bobbins with pointed ends, for easy sewings

Further reading:
Sue Thompson, *Introduction to Honiton Lace* (Batsford)
Elsie Luxton, *Technique of Honiton Lace* (Batsford)
Pat Perryman, *New Designs in Honiton Lace* (Batsford)

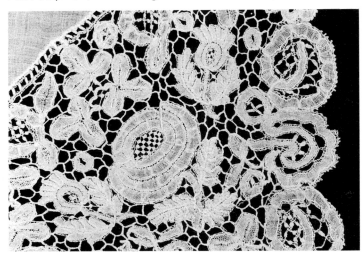

25. **Moira** locket design – a lesson in RH picots

8 prs – Brok 60

This very small design had to be simple and easy to finish – most of the little lockets it has been designed for have a ready-made backing – so you cannot cheat and sew through the backing with sewing needle and finish off behind!

It is made in two sections:

1. *Outside edge* is made complete; adding in pairs for flowers where shown; finish off and sew edge pairs before starting the

2. *Central flower*

Outside edge

Hang 1 pr at *A*, tw6 pin between at *B*.

Hang 1 pr on *B*, between first pr.

Braid and picot until *C*, hang 2 new prs round pin, tw2 both, ws both prs through braid prs and leave.

Braid and picot until *D*.

At *D* pin between braid prs, ws tw1 through each other, tw5 internal pr, take round pin *A*, separate threads to make twists stay in place – tw6 back to *D*, ws tw1 remove pin *B*, and replace between new prs.

See Diagrams *B*, *C* and *D*.

Repeat until *e*.

At *e*, *f* and *g*, pin between prs, tw1, continue; this makes a large hole for easy sewing into later.

When you get back to original pin *B*, sew 1 pr into *B*.

tw6 internal pr and tie off through all 6 loops left at central pin *A* (you will find it easier to do this in two moves).

Knot and cut off prs.

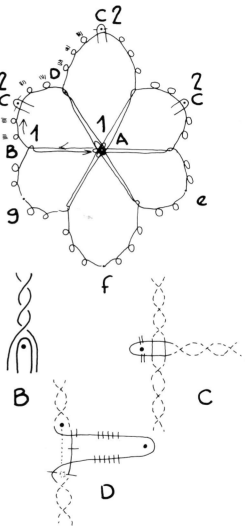

Outside edge

Central flower

Braid, pin and make leaves as shown.

Work 6 pair crossing No. 1 (see page 56).

Work 3 more leaves, pin and braid to edge.

Sew into enlarged holes and tie off.

Leave to set for 24 hours

Cut off ends leaving deliberate little ends as part of the design.

Central flower

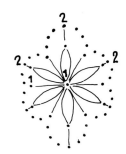

26. **Annette** paperweight or Christmas tree mobile

15 prs – Brok 60; 1 single gimp – DMC Coton Perlé 8

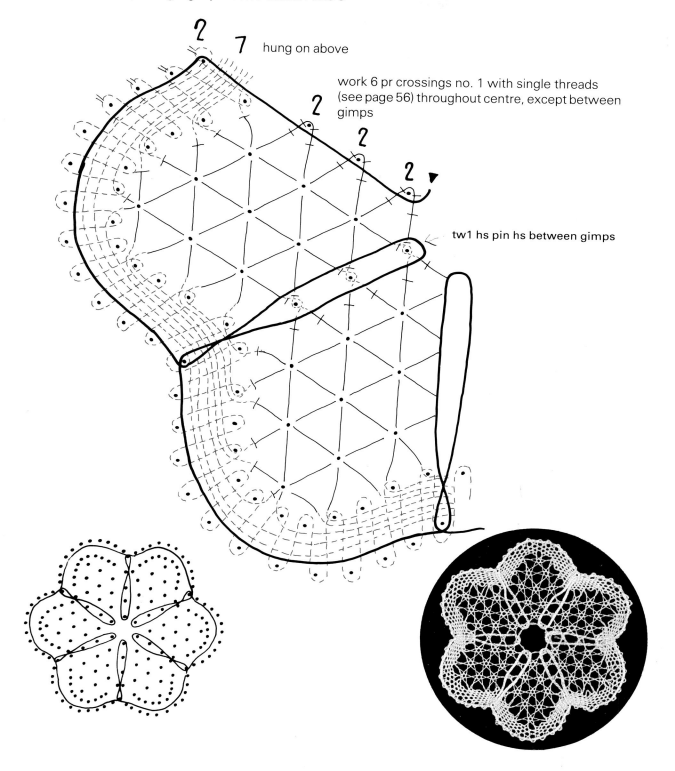

2
7   hung on above

work 6 pr crossings no. 1 with single threads (see page 56) throughout centre, except between gimps

2

2

2 ▶

tw1 hs pin hs between gimps

External corners survey

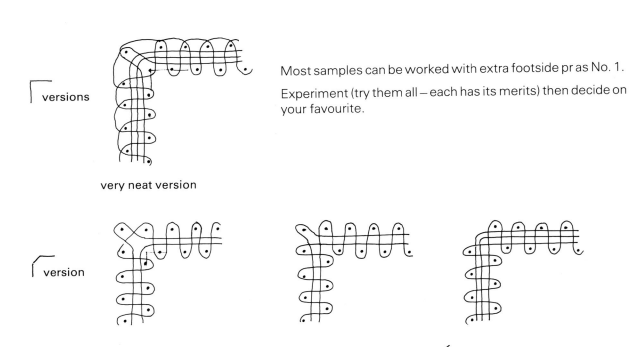

versions

very neat version

Most samples can be worked with extra footside pr as No. 1.

Experiment (try them all — each has its merits) then decide on your favourite.

version

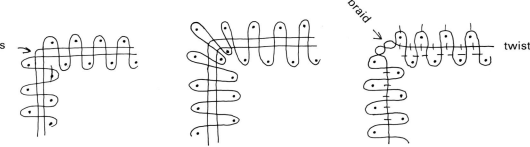

hs →

braid ↘

twist

pin used twice

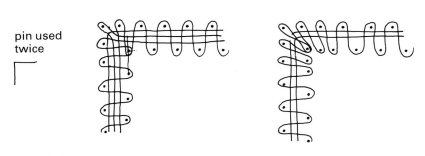

The choice all depends on (*a*) your pricking type,
(*b*) what suits your type of lace, (*c*) personal preference.

Internal corners survey

int. ext.

version

version

pin used
more than
once.

miscellaneous

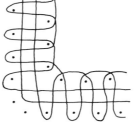

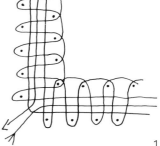

115

27. Butterfly in modern bobbin tape lace – a marvellous sewing exercise

7 prs wings; 8 prs body; 6 prs each flower – Bockens 50/2 Linen

27. Butterfly in modern bobbin tape lace
(cont.)

*7 prs wings; 9 prs body; 6 prs each flower – Bockens 50/2
Linen*

N.B. work wing section first; the body
is then worked and sewn on top.

1. tight bends: pin under one at
   outside edges, pin under two internally

2. less tight bend: instead of ws tw1
   after pin, take wpr *under* ppr

3. antennae: *ws tw1 outer edge prs, pin under 2,
   ws through 2 prs, tw1 wpr, leave and return with new
   wpr, 1 ws *; repeat from * to *

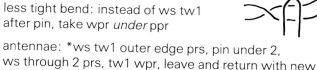

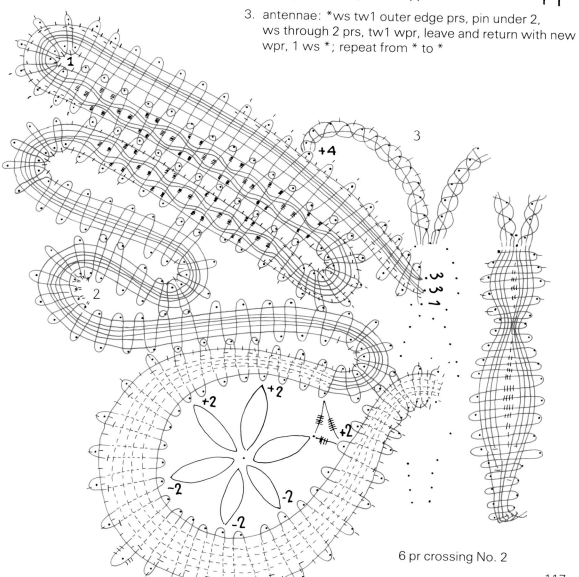

6 pr crossing No. 2

⅛″ or 3mm graph paper for drawing out Torchon sampler (page 70)

```
****************************************
*                                      *
*  **Lacemakers' golden rules**        *
*                                      *
*  Always use COVER CLOTHS — page 9    *
*                                      *
*  Worker cloth should NOT be MANMADE fibres — page 9 *
*                                      *
*  AVOID FRICTION with your threads, especially with *
*  your worker cloth — page 9          *
*                                      *
*  STROKE YOUR BOBBINS continually — page 17 *
*                                      *
*  NEVER touch your threads or work — page 13 *
*                                      *
*  WATCH YOUR WORK not your bobbins — page 13 *
*                                      *
*  TWIST BOBBINS not hand when hand winding bobbins *
*  — page 13                           *
*                                      *
*  HOLD your PASSIVES down while pulling wpr into *
*  position — page 30                  *
*                                      *
*  REPLACE PIN immediately AFTER SEWING — page 58 *
*                                      *
*  Practise settling twists round pin procedure until *
*  second nature — page 41             *
*                                      *
*  Mark thread spools if possible, or roll label up and put *
*  safe inside spool — I hate naked spools of thread!! *
*                                      *
****************************************
```

Books to read

General   Pamela Nottingham   — *The technique of bobbin lace* Batsford 1976
  — *Bobbin lacemaking* Batsford 1983

  Bridget M. Cook &   — *The book of bobbin lace stitches* Batsford 1980
  Geraldine Stott

Torchon   Pamela Nottingham   — *The technique of torchon lace* Batsford 1979

  Jennifer Fisher   — *Torchon lace for today* Dryad

Bedfordshire Pamela Robinson   — *A manual of Bedfordshire lace* Bean 1985
  Pamela Nottingham   — *The technique of bobbin lace* Batsford 1976

Bucks Point Geraldine Stott   — *A visual introduction to Bucks point lace* Batsford 1985

  Pamela Nottingham   — *The technique of Bucks point lace* Batsford 1981

  Geraldine Stott &
  Bridget M. Cook   — *100 traditional bobbin lace patterns* Batsford 1982

Honiton   Susanne Thompson   — *Introduction to Honiton lace* Batsford 1985

  Pat Perryman &
  Cynthia Voysey   — *New designs in Honiton lace* Batsford 1984

Modern   Ann Collier   — *Creative design in bobbin lace* Batsford 1982

Suppliers

United Kingdom

Alby Lace Museum
Cromer Road
Alby
Norfolk
NR11 7QE

Bedford Lace
4 Newnham Street
Bedford

Ann Brock
1 Ingham Close
Blake Hall Road
Mirfield
Yorkshire

Campden Needlecraft Centre
High Street
Chipping Campden
Gloucestershire

Chosen Crafts Centre
46 Winchcombe Street
Cheltenham
Gloucestershire
GL52 2ND

Margaret Clark
Mount Vernon
Lyme Road
Higher Poynton
Stockport
Cheshire
SK12 1TH

Leonie Cox
The Old School
Childswickham
Near Broadway
Worcs
WR12 7HD

J. and J. Ford
October Hill
Upper Way
Upper Longdon
Rugeley
Staffordshire
WS15 1QB

Framecraft
83 Hampstead Road
Handsworth Wood
Birmingham
B2L 1JA

Mr R. Gravestock
Highwood
Crews Hill
Alfrick
Worcestershire
WR6 5HF

Hepatica
82a Water Lane
Wilmslow
Cheshire

Frank Herring & Sons
27 High West Street
Dorchester
Dorset
DT1 1UP

Honiton Lace Shop
44 High Street
Honiton
Devon

D.J. Hornsby
149 High Street
Burton Latimer
Kettering
Northants
NN15 5RL

and
25 Manwood Avenue
Canterbury
Kent
CT2 7AH

Pastimes
24-6 West Street
Alresford
Hampshire

Jane's Pincushion
Wroxham Barns
Tunstead Road
Hoveton
Norwich
NR12 2QU

All branches of John Lewis

Lambourn Valley Cottage Industries
11 Oxford Street
Lambourn
Berks
RG16 7XS

Mace and Nairn
89 Crane Street
Salisbury
Wiltshire
SP1 2PY

Iris Martin
Farthing Cottage
Clickers Yard
Yardley Road
Olney
Bucks

Needle Work
Ann Bartlet
Bucklers Farm
Coggeshall
Essex
CO6 1SB

The Needlewoman
21 Needless Abbey
off New Street
Birmingham
B2 5AE

T. Parker
124 Corhampton Road
Boscombe East
Bournemouth
BH6 5NZ

Dorothy Pearce
5 Fulshaw Avenue
Wilmslow
Cheshire
SK9 51A

Jane Playford
North Lodge
Church Close
West Runton
Norfolk
NR27 9QY

Christine Riley
53 Barclay Street
Stonehaven
Kincardineshire
Scotland

Pat Savory
Tanglewood
4 Sanden Close
Hungerford
Berks
RG17 0LB

Peter and Beverley Scarlett
Strupak
Hill Head
Coldwells
Ellon
Grampian

Ken and Pat Schultz
134 Wisbech Road
Thornley
Peterborough

J.S. Sear
Lacecraft Supplies
8 Hill View
Sherrington
Buckinghamshire

Sebalace
Waterloo Mills
Howden Road
Silsden
W. Yorks
BD2 0HA

A. Sells
49 Pedley Lane
Clifton
Shefford
Bedfordshire

Shireburn Lace
Finkle Court
Finkle Hill
Sherburn in Elmet
N. Yorks
LS25 6EB

Stephen Simpson
Avenham Road Works
Preston
Lancs

Stitches
Dovehouse Shopping Parade
Warwick Road
Olton
Solihull
West Midlands

S.M.P.
4 Garner Close
Chalfont St Peter
Bucks
SL9 0HB

Teazle Embroideries
35 Boothferry Road
Hull
North Humberside

Valley House Crafts Studios
Ruston
Scarborough
N. Yorks

George Walker
The Corner Shop
Rickinghall
Diss
Norfolk

George White
Delaheys Cottage
Thistle Hill
Knareborough
N. Yorks
HG5 8LS

Bobbins
A.R. Archer
The Poplars
Shelland
Near Stowmarket
Suffolk
IP14 3DE

T. Brown
Temple Lane Cottage
Littledean
Cinderford
Gloucestershire

Bridge Bookshop
7 Bridge Street
Bath
Avon
B82 4AS

Cobwebs
Mary Johnson
80 Attimore Road
Welwyn Garden City
Hertfordshire

Stephen Cook
'Cottage Crafts'
6 Woodland Close
Flackwell Heath
Buckinghamshire
HP10 9EP

Chrisken Bobbins
26 Cedar Drive
Kingsclere
Newbury
Bucks
RG15 8TD

Malcolm J. Fielding
2 Northern Terrace
Moss Lane
Silverdale
Lancs
LA5 0ST

Richard Gravestock
Highwood
Crews Hill
Alfrick
Worcestershire
WR6 5HF

D.G. Harrison
27 Headingley Road
Rushden
Northants
NN10 0HS

Larkfield Crafts
Hilary Rickitts
4 Island Cottages
Mapledurwall
Basingstoke
Hants
RG25 2LU

Lambourn Valley Cottage Industries
11 Oxford Street
Lambourn
Berks
RG16 7XS

T. Parker
124 Corhampton Road
Boscombe East
Bournemouth
BH6 5NZ

Bryn Phillips
'Pantglas'
Cellan
Dyfed
Lampeter
SA48 8JD

D.H. Shaw
47 Zamor Crescent
Thruscroft
Rotherham
S. Yorks
S66 9QD

Sizelands
1 Highfield Road
Winslow
Bucks
MK10 3QU

Christine and David Springett
21 Hillmorton Road
Rugby
Warwickshire
CV22 5DF

Richard Viney
Unit 7
Port Royal Street
Southsea
Hants
PO5 4NP

George White
Delaheys Cottage
Thistle Hill
Knaresborough
N. Yorks

Lace pillows
Newnham Lace Equipment
15 Marlowe Close
Basingstoke
Hants
RG24 9DD

Books
Bridge Bookshop
7 Bridge Street
Bath
Avon
B82 4AS

Craft Bookcase
29 London Road
Sawbridgeworth
Herts
CM21 9EH

Christopher Williams
19 Morrison Avenue
Parkstone
Poole
Dorset
BH1Z 4AD

Silk embroidery and lace thread
E. and J. Piper
Silverlea
Flax Lane
Glemsford
Suffolk
CO10 7RS

Silk weaving yarn
Hilary Chetwynd
Kipping Cottage
Cheriton
Alresford
Hants
SO24 0PW

Frames and mounts
Doreen Campbell
'Highcliff'
Bremilham Road
Malmesbury
Wilts

Matt coloured transparent adhesive film
Heffers Graphic Shop
26 King Street
Cambridge
CB1 1LN

United States of America
Arbor House
22 Arbor Lane
Roslyn Hights
NY 11577

Baltazor Inc
3262 Severn Avenue
Metairie
LA 7002

Beggars' Lace
P.O. Box 17263
Denver
Colorado 80217

Berga Ullman Inc.
P.O. Box 918
North Adams
Massachusetts 01247

Frederick J. Fawcett
129 South Street
Boston
Massachusetts 02130

Frivolité
15526 Densmore N.
Seattle
Washington 98113

Happy Hands
3007 S.W. Marshall
Pendleton
Oregon 97180

International Old Lacers
P.O. Box 1029
Westminster
Colorado 80030

Lace Place de Belgique
800 S.W. 17th Street
Boca Raton
FL 33432

Lacis
2150 Stuart Street
Berkeley
California 9470

Robin's Bobbins
RTL Box 1736
Mineral Bluff
Georgia 30559

Robin and Russ Handweavers
533 North Adams Street
McMinnvills
Oregon 97128

Some Place
2990 Adline Street
Berkeley
California 94703

Osma G. Todd Studio
319 Mendoza Avenue
Coral Gables
Florida 33134

The Unique And Art Lace Cleaners
5926 Delman Boulevard
St Louis
Missouri 63112

Van Scriver Bobbin Lace
130 Cascadilla Park
Ithaca
New York 14850

The World in Stitches
82 South Street
Milford
N.H. 03055

Australia
Dentelles Lace Supplies
3 Narrak Close
Jindalee
Queensland 4074

The Lacemaker
94 Fordham Avenue
Hartwell
Victoria 3124

Spindle and Loom
Arcade 83
Longueville Road
Lane Cove
NSW 2066

Tulis Crafts
201 Avoca Street
Randwick
NSW 2031

Belgium
't Handwerkhuisje
Katelijnestraat 23
8000 Bruges
Belgium

Kantcentrum
Balstraat 14
8000 Bruges

Manufacture Belge de Dentelle
6 Galerle de la Reine
Galeries Royales St Hubert
1000 Bruxelles

Orchidée
Mariastraat 18
8000 Bruges

France
Centre d'Initiation à la Dentelle du Puy
2 Rue Duguesclin
43000 Le Puy en Velay

A L'Econome
Anne-Marie Deydier
Ecole de Dentelle aux Fuseaux
10 rue Paul Chenavard
69001 Lyon

Rougier and Ple
13-15 bd des Filles de Calvaire
75003 Paris

West Germany
Der Fenster Laden
Berliner Str 8
D 6483 Bad Soden
Salmunster

P.P. Hempel
Ortolanweg 34
1000 Berlin 47

Helkona De Ruijter
Kloeppelgrosshandel
Langer Steinweg 38
D4933 Blomberg

Holland
Blokker's Boektiek
Bronsteeweg 4/4a
2101 AC Heemstede

Theo Brejaart
Postbus 5199
3008 AD Rotterdam

Magazjin *De Vlijt*
Lijnmarkt 48
Utrecht

Switzerland
Fadehax
Inh. Irene Solca
4105 Biel-Benken
Basel

New Zealand
Peter McLeavey
P.O. Box 69.007
Auckland 8

Sources of Information
The Lace Guild
The Hollies
53 Audnam
Stourbridge
West Midlands
DY8 4AE

The Lace Society
Linwood
Stratford Road
Oversley
Alcester
Warwickshire
BY9 6PG

The British College of Lace
21 Hillmorton Road
Rugby
Warwickshire
CV22 5DF

The English Lace School
Honiton Court
Rockbeare
Nr Exeter
Devon

International Old Lacers
President
Gunvor Jorgensen
366 Bradley Avenue
Northvale
NJ 0766647
United States

United Kingdom Director of
International Old Lacers
S. Hurst
4 Dollius Road
London
N3 1RG

Ring of Tatters
Mrs C. Appleton
Nonesuch
5 Ryeland Road
Ellerby
Saltburn by Sea
Cleveland TS13 5LP

Museums
Bedford Museum
Castle Lane
Bedford
MK40 3XD

Cecil Higgins Museum & Art Gallery
Castle Close
Bedford
MK40 3NY

Luton Museum & Art Gallery
Wardown Park
Old Bedford Road
Luton
Bedfordshire
LU2 7HA

Index

abbreviations 10
adding-in 46
adding-in internally 88
Amanda pattern 86
Annette paperweight 113

basic pillow 9
Bedfordshire Lace 108
Bedfordshire trails 28, 84
bobbin carrier 20
bobbin lore 11
bobbin winder 36
bobbin winding 13
bias ground 72
block pillows 69
bookmarks
    Bluebell 54
    Crossroads 99
    Daisy 49
    Love-in-a-mist 52
    Lobelia 53
    spiders galore 55
    starting 48
    tops and tails 82
Brabant ground 52
braiding 19
braids/plaits/bars 29
buds 29
Bucks Point Lace 109
butterfly 116

carrying bags 20
changing workers 84
circular work 60, 113
colour coding 10, 15
continuous lace 28
corners
    designing 65
    external 114
    internal 115
    turning 64
cotton 38
crossings
    4-pair 32
    6-pair 56
    8-pair 74

crossroads bookmark 99

Daisy bookmark 49
drawing out 72
double zigzag 78

Eight-pair crossing 74
English laces 108
Ethel medallion 60
External corners 114

fans 29, 40, 48
Fir Tree fan 40
finishing 50, 62, 89
finishing off your hanky 68
footside 18
footside stitch 19
French fan lavender bag 87

getting ready 12
gimps 29, 46, 73, 79
'golden rules' 119
grounds or net 29

handy hints 30
hanging on horizontally 88
hanging on in order 24
hanging on in pairs 40
half spider 78
headside 29
Honiton Lace 110
hs and ws introduction 17
hs hanky, Amanda 86
hs trail 86

identifying traditional English laces 108-110
internal corners 115
in order, hanging on 24
in pairs, hanging on 40

Janice 76
June hanky 66

kiss stitch/changing workers 84
knot
    overhand 50
    reef 63

language of lace 29
lazy join 32
leaves 29
    modern 57
linen 39
Linette mobile 90
Lobelia bookmark 53
Love-in-a-mist bookmark 52

medallion, Ethel 60
mini bean-bag 30
mini spiders 53
mobile, Linette 90
modern prickings 22
Moira pendant 111
moving your lace/setting up 43
mushroom pillow 75
magic knot 81

needlelace 28
net or ground 29
Ninepin 32
non-continuous lace 28

pendant, Moira 111
photo sampler, Janice 76
picots
    simple 34
    survey 94, 95
pillows
    basic 9
    block 69
    labels 31
    mushroom 75
    summary 59
pincushion 44
pin talk 21
pin under one 18
pin under two 18
Poppies bookmark 24
pricker 12
pricking
    modern 22

proper 12
putting pillow to bed 20

rescue page 80, 81
rose grounds 53, 72, 78
Running River 84

setting up 43
sewings 58
silk 38
six-pair crossing 56
spiders 29, 48
Spiders Galore 55
starting
    bookmarks 48, 82
    straight 88
    general notes 63
straight finishes 89
straight starts 88
strivers 21

table settings 100-107
tallies 29, 73
temporary pinholes 24
thread thoughts 38
three-dimensional flowers 46
throwing out pairs 47, 80
Torchon
    ground 40
    lace 108
    sampler 70
tops and tails for bookmarks 82
trails 29
trail crossings 98
triangular ground 73
turning a corner 64
twists 17

veining 18

wall hanging 70
wedding bell 96
what lace? 28
winding bobbins 13
winkie pin 32
work sequence 23
ws and hs 16, 17

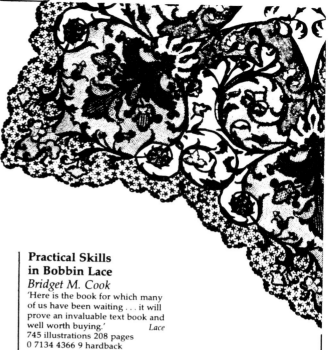